Dublin: The Chaos Years

Neil Cotter is Head of News at *The Irish Sun*. *Dublin: The Chaos Years* is his first book.

Dublin: The Chaos Years

*How the Dubs Made a Mess of
Things For So Long – and How
They Turned It Around*

NEIL COTTER

PENGUIN

IRELAND

PENGUIN IRELAND

UK | USA | Canada | Ireland | Australia
India | New Zealand | South Africa

Penguin Ireland is part of the Penguin Random House group of companies
whose addresses can be found at global.penguinrandomhouse.com.

First published 2018
001

Set in 13.5/16 pt Garamond MT Std
Typeset by Jouve (UK), Milton Keynes
Printed and bound in Great Britain by Clays Ltd, Elcograf S.p.A.

A CIP catalogue record for this book is available from the British Library

ISBN: 978–1–844–88431–5

www.greenpenguin.co.uk

MIX
Paper from
responsible sources
FSC
www.fsc.org   FSC® C018179

Penguin Random House is committed to a
sustainable future for our business, our readers
and our planet. This book is made from Forest
Stewardship Council® certified paper.

For Aoife, who gave me more leeway and encouragement
to do this than any Kerry person should, and Ted,
who'll stand on Hill 16 one day

Contents

Prologue

July 2009

The phone call lasted a few seconds.

Pat Gilroy was straight to the point. He was a busy man, and he had an All-Ireland quarter-final against Kerry to prepare for.

Earlier in the year he had sent young Diarmuid Connolly home from a training camp in La Manga for acting the maggot. Now, the player on the other end of the line was Mark Vaughan, the only player on the Dublin panel who could rival Connolly for raw talent. Vaughan had been spotted out on the lash. Phone calls were made, and the manager turned up to Café en Seine in Dawson Street to see his errant attacker – an equity trader by profession – enjoying a jar.

Vaughan did what anyone in his situation would do. He legged it from the pub.

'I was out having a few pints on a Friday evening,' he recalls. 'It was a work yoke, I had clients out with me. I was in a demanding job, and was actually injured anyway, just coming back into training. Someone saw me in Café en Seine, the barman texted his wife, I don't know a hundred per cent how it happened, but [Gilroy] just turned up. I was seen, so it couldn't be a "he said, she said" defence. I legged it. I ran.'

He could run, but he couldn't hide. 'I got a call the following day just to say "You're gone". That was it. No time for a chat, really.'

Vaughan was only twenty-four, but he had already been in and out of Dublin teams for four years. He was plagued by back injuries and played only a few minutes in Gilroy's first league campaign. The manager, who had taken over from Pillar Caffrey following a humiliating defeat to Tyrone in 2008, had no time to waste. When Vaughan asked for a break in the spring, Gilroy reluctantly gave him six weeks but warned him he wouldn't feature in the Leinster campaign. It was a poor start to a relationship that wouldn't last long.

Vaughan was back in training ahead of the Kerry match when he was busted, but Gilroy already had a fair idea of what the Kilmacud Crokes man was up to. His job involved bringing clients out. Going out meant pints. Pints meant the end.

'Put it this way, one of the lads who worked with us, his best friend was Gilroy's brother-in-law so he'd have known there was a good bit of that [corporate entertainment] in there,' Vaughan explained. 'I was probably too stubborn to apologize. I'm not sure he'd have taken me back anyway as there was a little bit of animosity from the start.'

Vaughan was hype, and Gilroy didn't appreciate hype. The new manager had seen how campaigns had been falling apart consistently since Dublin last won an All-Ireland in 1995. The blond bombshell was everything that was flash yet ultimately wrong about the Dubs machine. Stylish, not without substance, a free-taker – but prone to going missing when it mattered.

In the thirteen full seasons since a Dubs team containing a young Gilroy last claimed the Sam Maguire, they had failed to one degree or another thirteen times. They would fall again, and fall down hard: later in that summer of 2009, they would suffer further humiliation at the hands of Kerry. By this point, it was all so achingly familiar, so horribly predictable. As far as the viewing public could see, there was no All-Ireland in this team.

1. A Closed Shop

Mickey Whelan was ahead of his time, or so goes the accepted wisdom. In hindsight, he is seen as a 21st-century coach trapped in a 20th-century setting. A trainer with qualifications in 1996 was as rare as hens' teeth, and Whelan had the necessary certificates to put on the wall if he so chose.

The man was a GAA trailblazer, his whistle and stopwatch more educated than most. But was he genuinely ahead of his time in 1996? That depends on who is asked.

Whelan inherited a team that had just won the All-Ireland – but the players were arguably more marked by defeat than by victory. In 1991, they'd drawn Meath three times in the Leinster championship before finally losing the fourth match. In 1992, they'd been shocked by Donegal in the All-Ireland final. In 1994, they'd suffered the same fate at the hands of Down.

Defeat does strange things to good people. For this group of players, their view of the world was soured by bitter experience. John O'Leary, Mick Deegan, Charlie Redmond, Eamon Heery, Keith Barr, Paul Clarke, Paul Curran, Paul Bealin and Paddy Moran had worked like dogs in losing those games. So had Mick Kennedy, Gerry Hargan, Barney Rock and Kieran Duff before them. The Dublin jersey, though only a torch to be passed on, was jealously guarded. Now, almost all of these guys had All-Ireland medals – but that was not what drove their bitter attachment to the jersey.

Forget '95: none of these kids understood the pain of what went before. So they could get their hands off the jersey, because the jersey was going fucking nowhere.

The seasoned campaigners had their own dressing room at the Trinity College Sports Grounds in Santry, where Dublin trained in 1996. Facilities were rough and ready, bus routes limited, the welcome as cold and exposed as the complex itself. The dressing rooms were small, so space was at a premium.

Johnny Magee, a newcomer to the scene, remembers arriving on his first day. 'I walk in and Bealin is shouting: "Jaysus, lots of new faces here. It's like a revolving door, you see them come, you see them go" – and everyone having a laugh.' Magee would not make his league debut until the 1997 campaign, but he was around enough in '96 to see what was going on. He said: 'They were acting the bollox, they felt a little threatened, I suppose, with young lads coming in. They probably didn't realize their full potential, only winning one All-Ireland when they were good enough to win another two or three. Lads were apprehensive.'

His Kilmacud Crokes clubmate and fellow greenhorn Ray Cosgrove agrees. 'It was a little bit of a closed shop,' he says. 'Senior guys didn't welcome you with open arms. These were seasoned campaigners, wondering "Who's the young lad, does he think he's gonna come in and take my place?" It was very competitive but it was just some senior guys who felt under pressure. I don't think it was anything malicious, just lads who'd been there a long time who feared they were about to be pushed out.

'There was definitely a divide, new lads coming in would have to earn their respect. That wouldn't happen today, with Jim Gavin. If a new lad was coming into the squad, and senior guys were acting that way towards them? No way. It would be equal and open; but in 1996, with the lads who'd played in and won the All-Ireland, they were different. Different times.'

It didn't help that a new manager had been inflicted on this closed shop of old warhorses. For the summer of '96, Mickey Whelan was the man with the dubious honour of attempting a two-in-a-row with a squad who had been happy with their last boss. The dressing room was thus dominated by a cohort who didn't respect either the fresh legs coming in or the new manager with the new ideas.

Pat O'Neill was in his third season as manager when Dublin beat Tyrone in Croke Park on 17 September 1995. The players liked O'Neill, who managed almost by consensus, and they assumed he would remain. The team went away on their annual holiday, expecting to come back and pick up where they'd left off. Instead, O'Neill and his selectors walked. Tommy Lyons, the Mayo-born Crokes manager who had never played senior for Dublin, was told at one point the job was his. David Billings, a stalwart of Dublin GAA, was also under the impression he would be the man tasked with retaining the All-Ireland crown.

The Dublin County Board instead turned to Whelan, a St Vincent's man who had the blessing of his clubmate Kevin Heffernan, who won three All-Irelands as Dublin manager and held the mantle as the county's unofficial Godfather. Heffo's benediction was enough.

Whelan had won an All-Ireland as a player with Dublin while at the Clanna Gael club in 1963, and by 1995 had been mooted as a potential Dubs boss on and off for years. Yet he remained largely a curiosity, owing in part to a spell studying and playing soccer in the United States in the 1970s before returning to join Heffo's St Vincent's as a player. Whelan went on to help his adopted club to All-Ireland glory in 1976, but not before playing his own enormous part in the 1970s Dublin revival. He joined Heffernan's set-up as a coach ahead of the 1974 season, and quickly became known for his punishing training sessions involving laps, hills, and rows of tyres. The sessions – including, for the first time, work on a Saturday – were often brutal affairs that left Dublin, 33/1 outsiders for an All-Ireland that year, the fittest team in the land.

During his spell abroad, Whelan had done a Master's in physical education and biology at a college in West Virginia. In 1974, his insistence on a warm-up and cool-down was revolutionary. Whatever he did, it worked. Dublin, ignored by the experts and unloved by their own, went on to win their first All-Ireland title in eleven years. Whelan later returned to soccer, working under Jim McLaughlin and Dermot Keely with Dundalk FC. In the summer of 1995, as the Dubs were winning the All-Ireland, he had a fresh League of Ireland medal in his back pocket.

One of Whelan's first acts as Dublin boss was to tell the squad they were lucky to be All-Ireland champions. He also pinpointed the '95 full-back line – Ciarán Walsh especially – as one of the worst in history to win one. Maybe he was trying to be funny, or perhaps he was laying down a marker. Nobody could tell for certain. When he stopped running the players as hard as they were used to, and started training more with the football, suspicions immediately turned to frustration.

Dublin was a team that ran. They ran in the '70s, Whelan standing over them, whip in hand for some of it; they ran in the '80s; and they sure as hell weren't going to stop running in the '90s, having finally made it to the top of the tree.

The method to Whelan's perceived madness was simple. He wanted to make his players more comfortable on the ball, so that when bodies and minds were tired on match day, they would react positively while in possession. That meant drills with the ball, instead of without it. In 1996, that was an alien concept. The younger players embraced it; most of the older ones didn't.

Keith Barr, who had taken over as captain from John O'Leary, reckons the new man's training methods were no more advanced than what you might see in club nurseries on a Saturday afternoon.

'Mickey Whelan was a good man and a decent manager, but he was absolutely not ahead of his time,' he says. 'He always wanted to use the ball in exercises, but drills with the ball were primitive. We'd be in a square, the type you'd see at juvenile level. The principle was to use the ball, but for me it wasn't scientific. It didn't say you were better running 200 metres with the ball than 200 metres without.

'He did it no better than Pat, just different. He was entitled to train with the ball more often. Either it works or it doesn't. Pat had more of a balance, but doctors differ and patients die. It was a different way of getting fit. You can bring the horse to water but it might not drink at all.'

Eamon Heery believes Whelan should never have taken the job, but he didn't know how to say no. The St Vincent's player had dropped off the Dublin panel following a dispute with management, and missed out on an All-Ireland medal. His old mentor at club level asked him back in 1996, and he jumped at it. But everything had changed by then.

'Lads were acting the bollox. Fellas playing together for so long, they had put in some graft and they were tired. It was a flagging team, and Mickey made a mistake getting involved with them, as the nucleus of that team was totally bolloxed. The training that had been done, which I was part of under [Paddy] Cullen and O'Neill, was fucking savage. By the time it went to '95 a lot had nothing left. Mickey went to pick it up but it just wasn't there, you know? And once they'd won an All-Ireland in '95 they were kinda going "Fuck this".'

Heery never spoke publicly about why he missed out on that medal. He can live with it, and only regrets missing out on the feeling he imagines he'd have had in the immediate aftermath of the final whistle. Otherwise, he couldn't give a damn.

'I wasn't there, end of, the lads won,' he says. 'I got a phone call off Jim Gavin after they won in '95, which was amazing. He was a young guy, it was huge. I don't know why he did it but it was amazing to get it and I have great respect for him for it. There was no animosity with the players. Yes, one hundred per cent I'd love to have won it, but I didn't. I've a wife, two healthy children and that's more important.

'I would have loved that ten seconds of "yes" – I would have loved that, I missed that. But other than that, shit happens.'

He reckons in hindsight that Whelan should have left him on the scrapheap in 1996, along with some other former greats he reintroduced to the panel. 'Mickey didn't know when to say fucking no and sometimes you have to say no. That team was fading, and then you bring back myself, Joe McNally and Niall Guiden, I'd say that went down a fucking treat with the lads. I didn't give a fuck – I was just delighted to go back and see if I could compete with these guys again, and I did OK. It could have been a mistake in respect of the guys that were there. He may have said, "I'd like to bring you back, Eamo, but in light of everything I can't," and I'd have said, "I hear ya."

'Guys were mentally and physically fucked. When Mickey took over, rightly or wrongly, he was pulling off tricks, telling them their stats were up to, in order to try and get their heads right! When it was clear guys weren't going at a hundred per cent after they'd won the All-Ireland. There was a serious lack of motivation.'

The older players did what they could to make life uncomfortable for the new arrivals, while keeping themselves amused. Imac hair-removal cream in the bottle of Head & Shoulders was a big favourite, as was rubbing Deep Heat in some fella's jocks just before a big team meeting.

On one occasion, six of the stalwarts took a newbie to breakfast in a café on Abbey Street after training one Saturday morning. They told him this was one of the perks of playing for your county: lots of free meals around town. 'We had the full Irish,' says one of them, more than two decades later. 'Orange juice. And another round of brekkies. And tea, lovely. Then one of the lads has to pop out, and another. Two more say they'll be back in a sec. Then the other two go out to find the rest of them. We all line up across the road to watch as the waitress approaches the young fella and hands him the bill. He tried to explain that the county board was looking after it, and she says, "The what?" He gets frantic at the prospect of a monster bill, looks out and we're falling around the street, laughing. Poor bastard.'

Charlie Redmond was the squad's joker-in-chief. His colleagues often tell the story that when Whelan brokered a boot deal with Adidas, the Puma-wearing free-taker took his new £150 pair despite having no intention of wearing them. He asked his wife to bring them into a sports shop, tell them he'd bought them a while back but they didn't fit, and get a refund. The same thing had, apparently, worked for Mick Deegan a few days before. According to legend, the boots weren't even due to go on sale to the public until the following week. True or not, it became part of Charlie's folklore.

Barr had been around since 1989. He understands why he and his fellow Dublin veterans were seen as a difficult group. Whenever that seed was planted, he was there to watch it germinate.

'Defeat hardens you. If people did come in after '95, and they have a view of it being an unwelcoming dressing room, and if I was being particularly unwelcoming to them, I fully accept their view. I cannot dispute or deny it,' he says.

'That was a team that had played three All-Ireland finals, had lost against Donegal, Down, Derry in a semi-final. That team was going back to '88 when we played Meath and lost in a Leinster final, and then you had Cork in '89 when we lost in an All-Ireland semi-final and then Meath again in 1990. It was a hardened team, a hardened group of players. Defeat in a final or in a big game hardens you.'

Until 2001, the provincial and All-Ireland championships were played on a pure knockout basis. One defeat and you're out. No second chances. This was one of the reasons that players weren't developed over a number of seasons – they either did it when their chance arrived, or they faded into obscurity. It was not a fertile environment for personal or professional growth. And it certainly wasn't conducive to cosy dressing-room atmospheres.

'Always remember, the modern-day player today has two bites at the fucking apple,' Barr says. 'When we were playing, it was knockout, winner took all, there was no room for losers. We played Meath in '91, there were four matches. There were a quarter of a million people there. They didn't come to see soft people. They didn't come to see people with soft attitudes. It was winner take all. It was gladiator against gladiator. You were in the Coliseum. That was my perspective.'

Sticking around for a prolonged period of time in the inter-county set-up was, in 1995, a considerable achievement. The bonds between the players who hung in were solid. They were there because they had proven they could do it, not because they had the potential. Potential rarely came into it in senior inter-county football. What can you do for us now? If you're bringing nothing to the table, I'm sorry, but can you please get off that chair?

Magee agrees with Barr's assessment of the pre-qualifier era. There was no margin of error, no room for experiment. 'One bad performance in championship, that could be your county career over if you didn't adjust to it or play well. If you've a bad day, will you be brought back in? If you play badly for whatever reason, you mightn't get another one. It was pretty cut-throat in that sense.'

Whelan could be cut-throat too. He was not afraid to get rid of faces that didn't fit. He was handed a three-year deal and was determined to do things his own way, at least initially.

Paul Clarke was one of Dublin's stand-out performers in 1995. The wing forward was a player, full of self-belief, who felt at the top of his game. He was one of the first to face Whelan's axe, and would watch the 1996 Leinster final against Meath from Hill 16, with other outcasts, Ciarán Walsh and the highly regarded Vinnie Murphy.

Clarke, like most of the players from that era, can reel off the big days like he's listing the alphabet. He says: 'We'd gone through a right tough decade. There were a lot of old legs, a lot of mileage, we put in a serious shift in training in '95, I couldn't see us not winning it, and we did. All the hope was Pat would stay on and manage the team, and I felt there was a new lease of life. We had seven All-Stars on that All-Ireland winning team, which says you're at the top of your game.'

O'Leary, Curran, Barr, Brian Stynes, Dessie Farrell, Clarke and Redmond picked up gongs that year. They were names that rolled off the tongue. It would be four years before another player from the capital – the brilliant Ciaran Whelan – became an All-Star.

Whelan's appointment gave Clarke a chance to impress a new man, but the new man was slow to take to him. 'Mickey wanted to lay down his marker. When he came in there was a bit of a shock, he wanted to change things up a lot, brought in players; he gave an opinion on what he thought of us, and what he thought of us winning an All-Ireland. For some of us it was very hard to take. I personally got a bit of a roasting. But that wasn't going to stop me, I had an All-Ireland medal and an All-Star and I had had a brilliant season, and was determined to win another one of these.

'But he told me I was burned out and needed a break, even though I felt the contrary. He was the manager, you respect your manager no matter what. That's the problem these days, people tend to get into huddles and have them sacked, but he was the boss so I had to do whatever I had to do to get back into the team.'

Dublin's league form in 1995/6 was average, four wins and three defeats in Division 2 – leaving them fifth behind Cork, Cavan, Armagh and Leitrim. For some of the players, it was too easy to compare the new guy to the last guy. Whelan wanted them to cast off the shackles and attack, but they didn't want the freedom he was offering. It was only after O'Neill left did it become clear that his charges had become institutionalized. They were standing at the gates with a key in their hand and a sleeping guard at their mercy. But nobody took the leap.

Fans were energized by the return of Heery and Guiden, and by the shock reappearance of Joe McNally, the roly-poly 1983 All-Ireland winner and All-Star who hadn't seen action with the Dubs for quite a while. Young lads floated round the fringes too, but it wasn't exactly a new beginning for a tired team. Out with the old, in with the older.

Heffernan was a surprise traveller with the team when Dublin launched their Leinster campaign against Westmeath in Navan on 9 June 1996. The Dubs strolled to a 1-18 to 0-11 win. Redmond was back where he'd left off the previous year, hitting five points, while centre-back Barr got the goal. The returning McNally scored 0-3, Heery and Guiden also hitting the target.

Three weeks later they were back in Navan – Heffo once more as a travelling companion – where they saw off Louth by 1-9 to 0-8 in the semi-final. Redmond again got 0-5, McNally 1-1, Gavin, Bealin and Guiden a point each.

Next up, in the Leinster final, was Meath. Dublin had hammered Meath in the 1995 Leinster final, perhaps the highlight of their march to the title. Some 63,000 spectators watched the Dubs dismantle their young rivals in sun-baked Croke Park, with Redmond and Farrell picking them off ruthlessly like trained assassins. Clarke's fisted goal and Jason Sherlock's smacker on referee Pat Casserly were highlights in the 1-18 to 1-8 trouncing. After the game the squad went out on one of their legendary drinking sessions, and were in Bad Bob's in Temple Bar when they bumped into one of the Meath players. Colleagues recall that words were exchanged, and then it escalated. Blood was spilled and one member of the Dublin contingent ended up being ushered out the back door by bouncers.

Fast forward to 28 July 1996 in the same sporting venue. In a turgid affair wrecked by heavy rain, Dublin led with ten minutes to go by two points but were overrun by a late four-point rally. No Meath team had beaten the reigning All-Ireland champions in more than thirty years, despite going head to head with many over the decades. Their 0-10 to 0-8 win launched the Royals to All-Ireland glory in September.

The Dublin players were meeting up to pore over the year that was. But, perhaps symptomatic of the malaise that had set in, they failed to find a fault with anyone other than Whelan.

Dublin was an old team. A glance at the starting line-ups tells its own story.

DUBLIN: O'Leary 35, Moran 29, Deasy 36, Deegan 32, Curran 27, Barr 28, Heery 32, Stynes 25, Bealin 29, Whelan, 20, Gavin 25, Redmond 32, Gilroy 25, Sherlock 20, Farrell 25.

MEATH: Conor Martin 24, Mark O'Reilly 19, Darren Fay 20, Martin O'Connell 32, Colin Coyle 33, Enda McManus 24, Paddy Reynolds 19, Jimmy McGuinness 22, John McDermott 26, Trevor Giles 21, Tommy Dowd 26, Graham Geraghty 23, Evan Kelly 22, Brendan Reilly 27, Barry Callaghan 20.

At just 23, Graham Geraghty had already lost more than his fair share of games against Dublin. Coming in to 1996, however, he felt that a combination of the Dubs' advancing years and a new vitality in the Royals set-up under 1987 and 1988 All-Ireland winning manager Seán Boylan, was about to reap dividends.

'Things got rejigged, we brought in minors and U21s, and we worked very hard,' he says. 'Going out at the start of '96 nobody gave Meath a chance because we had a mediocre league campaign. The first round of the championship was against Carlow and I remember my wife saying to me, "You will probably get beaten today", because we weren't going well. But confidence was high within the camp. Training was going well, we didn't think we'd win an All-Ireland but there was a good buzz in the camp. I actually remember that morning, I said to her going out the door, "We'll win the All-Ireland." Whether it was in jest or not I don't know!

'There was a confidence, a lot of young players who'd won at under-age level and knew what it took to win, but with every game we got better and better. We had five lads in from minor, Dubs had five in their thirties. We had no inkling of any problems in their camp. Dublin are probably masters at hiding what's going on; it's only after that you think there must be something up. But when everyone isn't pulling in the same direction there will be problems. That happened for Dublin.'

Dessie Farrell was an All-Star and was being spoken about as the worthy successor to 1970s' lynchpin Tony Hanahoe on the 40. He was nominated for the GAA Writers' Player of the Year award in 1995. So when they went to play Meath, he was positioned in the corner. Other than the introduction of Raheny man Ciaran Whelan for the injured Guiden, there was nothing new or slick about how Dublin's forward line looked. Young Ray Cosgrove was shooting the lights out in the A v. B games, and many within the camp were predicting he would start against the Royals. In the end, the Kilmacud man didn't even make the subs bench.

Asked about that time, Cosgrove recalls: 'I was top scoring, young, flying it, but it was Meath so it might have been a big risk. I still believe by [my] not even getting a jersey that day, [Mickey Whelan] was succumbing to the senior guys. I was very close, but Whelan was definitely influenced by the senior players at that stage.'

Did the players hold the power? It depends on who's asked. Clarke would spend hours talking with Whelan, trying to improve, fitting in with the new man's methods. A less committed player than Clarke would have walked away when a fourteen-year-old fan was drafted in to play a practice game in the lead-up to the Meath game. The fan was young Wayne McCarthy, a familiar face at training who would later play for Dublin for real. Wayne was known to the entire panel and would act as ball boy for Redmond as he popped over free after free. Committed a supporter as the young lad was, it's unlikely he was quite ready for the cut and thrust of Leinster final action.

Clarke recalls that in the run-up to the Leinster final, he didn't make the starting 15 for a challenge match. 'I went, "OK, I'm not quitting now." Then they played a 15 v. 15, players were brought in from clubs and I didn't even make the second 15. I was brought on as a sub late on in that trial match. I saw the writing on the wall. Come championship, a few of us got a rude awakening. When he was naming the team and the subs for the first round, we didn't even make the subs, and then you were told "Well, we don't need you at training for the next couple of nights, we just want to train with the team and the subs." It was felt we would be bringing a negative vibe or aura because we weren't playing.

'Ciarán [Walsh], Vinnie [Murphy] and myself were on the Hill supporting the team, ready to get back into training on the Tuesday night. I wanted to play and that was that, I was in great shape. I felt fit and strong, no one was telling me otherwise. I could have rode off into the sunset but no, I wanted to prove people wrong and prove to myself I had the heart and the fight for it.'

He spoke with the manager: 'Tell me what you need me to do and I'll do it.'

'I love training,' Clarke says. 'Fran Ryder used to put together the training sessions in Pat O'Neill's time, and I thought he was great. Whenever Fran was through I'd ask him, was there any more. Mickey is a very strong personality, and had an incredible pedigree. He'd been away and studied in America, he brought in new training methods. I thought, "Brilliant, new ideas, throw it at me," because I enjoy all of that.

'I sat down with Mickey a number of times and said, "What do I have to do?" I thought by doing that, it was going to help my cause because I was open to finding out what I needed to do, and I did follow his instructions, what he wanted me to do, but maybe my face didn't fit, that's how it goes, you know?'

Clarke, who would later go into coaching himself, says that Whelan's methods did not strike him as particularly revolutionary. 'Fran was a great trainer, ahead of his time also. So it wasn't rocket science when Mickey came in, we were sort of au fait with a lot of it. I had a training background anyway, I was an instructor and always kept up to date with methods so I wasn't blown away.'

Whelan, to Clarke's mind, 'was too quick to break up the '95 team. I have to be honest. Look at Meath: we beat them by 10 points in '95 and they won the All-Ireland in '96. What's that about? Did they all of a sudden reinvent the wheel? Or is it that we dropped a level or two, and once we were out of the way Meath had an easy run in?'

Others resisted the will of the new man. It worked for some and didn't for others. The new players coming in didn't know what to make of the dynamic that had taken hold. Imagine, you're a young player taking your first tentative steps into the senior set-up. You've watched and read about these men from afar, dreaming that one day you'll join their ranks. And then once you're in, they don't seem to be following the code of conduct you'd envisaged. Whatever happened to obeying the manager?

Nobody was sure which direction was the right one, never mind whether they were all travelling it together. Barr, O'Leary and Redmond were seen as the leaders of the dressing room, men who had earned the respect of everybody. Difficult men, when they didn't know you or care whether you were even there or not.

Cosgrove remembers: 'We hadn't got respect at that stage. We were training in Trinity. You'd have the senior lads in their dressing room. Fellas like Paddy Moran and Davy Byrne, the sub goalie, were good fellas. Mick Deegan would go about his business quietly. Dessie and Paul Curran would have no animosity towards you. Mickey was probably a little too nice to some of the senior guys, on reflection. He probably should have culled a few of them, clipped their wings, because they were having a massive influence around the place.'

Magee says, 'There seemed to be a lack of respect towards Mickey from senior players. He'd be saying stuff, some lads would be skitting. It seemed to me when I went in, whatever happened throughout '96, there was something like a hangover had kicked in. I knew there was something up. You could sense some of the senior players weren't with him. They'd do the training but, I felt, fellas did their own thing.'

Darren Homan was another young man brought in for 1996. The Tallaght man was a scrapper, a no-nonsense midfielder not afraid to put it about. He wasn't shy and was never afraid to take the head off an opponent – and legend had it that he didn't necessarily limit it to opponents. But he respected his manager, and he felt some of the established players didn't afford the same courtesy.

'Mickey Whelan was very unfortunate. The team was age-ing, the lads weren't putting in as much of an effort as they had over the years,' he says. 'They were doing the dog on it, celebrating and all that. He wanted to put his own stamp on it, bring a bit of youth in, because when he came on board the lads had won their All-Ireland, they were out celebrating most of the time, so he kind of had to start again. Was the respect not there? That would be fair to say.

'Mickey had us doing what we'd call strange training at the time, but what he'd learned in the USA hadn't reached Ire-land yet! Lads were used to doing laps of Santry in the previous regime and thought it was strange what he was doing.'

Barr's influence ran deepest. He didn't put his arm around new lads' shoulders. His door wasn't always open. Get your boots on, and get out on the pitch. Prove to me that you're good enough to share this fucking dressing room. He might not have been rolling out the red carpet for younger players, but he wasn't slamming the door in their faces either – if they were good enough.

'Always remember we had two young lads who won All-Irelands in '95,' he says. 'Jason [Sherlock] and Keith Galvin. In their first year they won an All-Ireland for Dublin. I didn't have a problem with them, because the reality of sport is they were no threat to my position. And welcome to sport, it's dog eat dog. That's the reality. You're not going to come in and put your arm around the young fella and say, "By the way, there's my jersey, you're a great player." What you're going to say to him is, "You're in and you want my jersey? Come and fucking get it." That's the reality of sport. I'm sorry it's not posh enough for you.'

Homan settled quickly in that kind of environment, and he felt welcomed. It helped that he was a huge man with an attitude to match. He says: 'I was a little wilder then! I came with a bit of a reputation, I was a little bolder when younger, and had served a suspension or two. When I got involved the lads never really gave me any trouble, they were great. Eamon Heery was great encouragement, most of the lads were.' There was perhaps one exception: 'Barrsy would want his position, and would want nobody at all challenging for it!'

Heery didn't feel like he was going out of his way to be nice to the younger lads. He doesn't believe that just saying hello to a fella before training should mark him out as a hero. 'The thing about Johnny [Magee], I like him,' he says. 'He was from Stillorgan but he wasn't a Stillorganite, if you get me. Homan, a guy I liked so it made no odds. Johnny was a good, honest, decent person, came from a good family. What's the point in being nasty to someone? OK, if the cunt is coming in to take your position, fight like fuck, but other than that? I tried to keep to myself, keep my head down and see if I could compete again with these guys. It took nothing to be nice to guys. If some of these fucking clowns thought they were great because they won one All-Ireland, well then shame on them.

'They would never dare do it to me. I always got on well with the majority, they didn't have to be your best friend, but I respected them and got on with them. This is no disrespect to the new guys coming in but when I came in there was Mick Kennedy and Barney [Rock], these guys, and you had to make them like you. These are the main fucking men, it's up to you.

'Most of them I liked anyway, it was great to be with them, but it might have been a mentality from the other [new or returning] guys – "They don't want me." They don't want me? I don't fucking care. Some of the lads coming in weren't good enough, possibly. And some of the '95 crew would have been saying also, "What the fuck is Heery doing back?" I didn't get it to my face, but possibly behind my back. I was very close with Keith and Paddy Moran, and if they were sleeveen enough I would have heard it back through Keith or Paddy.'

Barr hears former players talk about their experiences of closed shops, and rifts, and dressing-room divides. He hears people say that's not the case today, and he calls bullshit on all of it. 'You hear Declan Darcy say the next fella could win you an All-Ireland so you put your arm around him, but the reality is that doesn't happen behind the scenes.

'When you're in dressing rooms and in camps, we trained many times A v. B and there was riots at it. There were fights. Pub-crawl fights, you know what I'm trying to say? That's the reality, and people don't see that. But what happens today now is those realities do happen to a certain extent but people don't speak about them. Everything is hush hush, closed down, all training sessions today are behind closed doors. Lock and key. Ours were open, people could walk in off the street, we had people coming down watching on a regular basis. Whatever happened, they saw it. Don't get me wrong, it wasn't a weekly occurrence. It happened at a specific time of the season. You could go out and draw a Leinster final, and you could be playing in two weeks' time. Well the next two weeks were going to be very fucking tense. Players are highly intelligent people, they're not dunces, they know if you play bad on a particular day or match, the managers are going to make changes. So that player now has two weeks to prove himself. Two weeks to go back to the manager. Through body language, team meetings, players would give their opinion, and they were like salesmen. Trying to sell themselves. *Pick me, boss, I'm the man for it.*

'I never knocked on anybody's door. I believe I was good and entitled to be picked. I always knew, though, if you didn't play well you wouldn't be fucking picked.'

The leading lights in that Dublin squad were driven, fiercely competitive but also selfish men. Sure, it was all about the team. But at the crucial moments, nobody was more important than the individual who wanted a jersey with a number 15 or lower on it. They won and lost together, and they partied hard together, but when backs were to the wall, it was every man for himself. Once that was established, it was time to die for the cause.

Barr puts it this way: 'I had three big mates in the squad: Keith Barr, Keith Barr and Keith Barr. Not one of those put their arms around my shoulder! But I had a fair and good relationship with them all. Because of your position, my close friends would be defenders. A phenomenal friend, a phenomenal player, was Eamon Heery. I was very close to Curraner. What do I mean by that? I haven't seen him in three fucking years or spoken to him once in that time, but it doesn't lessen my respect for him, and that's life. John O'Leary was great, Mick Kennedy, Gerry Hargan, wonderful guys. Another great friend of mine, a phenomenal player who never got the credit, was Paddy Moran, a gentleman, great craic. I was great friends with Dessie and Mick Galvin. Charlie, a fellow clubman of mine, is a wonderful lad and great craic. There's always the devil in Charlie. I had a ball with every one of those players and that was genuine. The craic over the years was mighty.'

Barr understood his possessiveness of his jersey in terms of historical obligation. He wondered whether some of the newer faces appreciated that.

'It's my duty as a Dublin footballer to pass on that jersey

and pass on that jersey the way I got it from great men of the '70s and '80s,' he says. 'I got it from those people and it was handed down to me. When players say it's a cosy and lovely environment, I call them spoofers and losers. Anybody who played at that level knows that when the doors are closed, they say go get them boys, don't hold back. Cork, Down, Meath. We would have had a great rivalry with Meath, a great respect, Kildare were flying at that time.

'We knew Kildare were a talented side managed by a great manager in Micko, with a lot of finance coming in at the time. They were a county that meant business and they weren't coming to Croke Park to make up numbers. It's like a rebellion: you have to crush it. You don't crush it by being nice, or by putting your arms around somebody's shoulder. Because you know, when you join the army, yes you have to have manners and be a gentleman but when you're called upon to do your job in the special forces, you fucking do it. And when you have your foot on their throat, you don't take it off. That's what elite sports is about and anyone who tells you different is a spoofer.'

Barr was one of the players who didn't want to see the back of O'Neill. But he wasn't too concerned when Whelan came in and told the players they'd been lucky to win an All-Ireland. 'It didn't bother me, it was only other players picked up on it. They said: "He said we were lucky to win an All-Ireland!" and I said: "Were we not?!" We won an All-Ireland, and I didn't necessarily disagree! I said, "Let's get down to business, lads. I want to win my second and my third."'

At the end of the 1996 season, county board chairman John Bailey had a message for the board: John O'Leary had told him that the players backed the manager. O'Leary would later claim he hit the roof when he heard, insisting in his autobiography that he told Bailey nothing of the sort.

Whelan began to come under serious fire during the following league campaign. The Dubs finished third in Division 2, winning just three of their seven games. His fate was effectively sealed, even if nobody appreciated it fully at the time, when Leitrim secured their first ever competitive win over Dublin on 13 October 1996, winning by 1-10 to 0-10. Draws with Armagh and Mayo followed before Dublin edged a win against Clare. The Parnell Park boo boys let him know how they felt in defeat to Louth before they finished the campaign with victories over Monaghan and already-promoted Laois. Dublin fans began to wonder what might have been when Tommy Lyons's Offaly went on to wrap up the league title.

Dublin's season ended at the first Championship hurdle, when they were drawn against Meath. They were watched by the reigning world snooker champion, Ken Doherty, who received the biggest cheer of the day when parading his new trophy on the Croke Park pitch.

The Dublin team included twelve starters from the 1995 final, with the same six forwards back on display. If 1996 was about breaking them up, 1997 was about putting them back together. Whelan seemed to be running out of ideas.

A 1-9 to 0-1 blitz in the first half left Dublin on the brink of humiliation. But the Dubs rallied after half-time, summoning guts from the vast reserves built up over the previous decade and operating on muscle memory, almost making it. With the last kick of the game, Bealin smashed a penalty against the crossbar.

Defeat spoiled what for Clarke would have been a victory for stubborn determination. He made it off Hill 16 and back on to the pitch for one last hurrah – as, interestingly enough, did Ciarán Walsh. It wasn't the fairy tale he'd sweated for. Maybe Whelan was right, perhaps he was spent. Or maybe he just had a bad day. But he failed to make an impact, and his Dublin career fizzled out at the hands of younger, fresher opponents.

'I got started against them, but it was one of those days,' he says. 'I didn't have a good day, one of the young lads gave me a lesson I would have given other Meath players before. He had a good game, I was taken off, the boys were beaten and that was it. That was my career pretty much over then.'

Whelan had promised to walk away if Dublin failed to make it past the first round, but, seemingly emboldened by the heroic near-recovery, he decided to stay on and hope nobody bothered bringing up his pre-match vow.

Few of the players were going to forget Whelan's promise. They blamed him for the mess they were in, to the extent that by the time the league resumed some were operating on automatic pilot. Nothing the lame-duck manager said stuck. The players were going to do their own thing. For youngsters newly introduced on to the panel, that much was obvious.

Dublin lost the league opener away to Sligo, a late goal condemning them to an embarrassing 2-7 to 0-12 defeat on 19 October. Whelan, targeted throughout by the travelling supporters, struggled to come to terms with one of his worst defeats yet.

After the game, goalkeeper Davy Byrne, struggling to find something positive to say, could do no better than this: 'We scored more times than Sligo but they got two goals in the last few minutes which proved decisive. Fair play to them they took them well, even though there was an element of luck about the second one.'

Offering platitudes in defeat to minnows was not where Dublin wanted to be. The county board had a decision to make, even if that meant not really making a decision. Never in the county's history had a manager been sacked after one league game. They erred on the side of caution. There would be no panic, although requests were made on the quiet to start drawing up a list of names just in case that time came. Offaly were up next in Parnell Park. Surely it couldn't get any worse.

2. Civil War

Mickey Whelan, a Dublin man to the tips of his toes, was ashen-faced as he walked off the Parnell Park pitch. Dublin had lost again, this time to Offaly by 1-11 to 1-8 in the National League. He'd heard the insults before, most notably after the previous defeat, against Sligo, when some supporters hurled cans at him. But this was worse, much worse. This wasn't just the usual drunken idiots roaring invective.

The medicine that this man of science had prescribed for his patient wasn't going down well, and like vexed relatives in a hospital ward the crowd took it out on him. One twelve-year-old girl managed to make herself heard above the boos. 'You should be ashamed of yourself,' she told him, as a bar of chocolate hurtled towards his head from another, unseen assailant. Whelan, hurrying from the pitch just a few hundred yards from the St Vincent's club where he was revered, had already made up his mind to walk away.

'No one died,' he told the media as he left the Parnell Park dressing room. But it felt a bit like a funeral, or an execution.

Up in the stands, another Dublin great struggled to take in what he was seeing. Tommy Carr knew all about losing with the Dubs over a ten-year playing career. He knew how to win too, but the losses seemed to stick out. The former county skipper retired in 1994 following the All-Ireland final defeat to Down. He did it quietly, no pints with the lads, no fuss. Some might not even have noticed he was gone until the league came back, around a few months later.

He was in Parnell Park on Sunday, 2 November 1997, as a fan, only occasionally thinking about the medal that got away. The players were making their way across the pitch to the dressing room, but everyone had eyes only for Mickey. Eamon Heery – a St Vincent's clubmate and a player Whelan had brought back from the wilderness – stuck his finger up at the crowd. Shut the fuck up, he was telling them. Have some respect.

Watching the scene, Carr felt both sorrow and anger. 'Mickey was my minor coach so I would have known him quite well,' he says. 'I still remember the figure of him walking across the pitch and the boos ringing out, the various cat cries, and I felt sorry for him. He wouldn't be a guy who deserved that because he poured his heart and soul into Dublin football and Vincent's football,' he says.

Carr, then thirty-six, was still playing club football with Lucan Sarsfields and had no football management experience. But he reckoned he could coach, if someone would give him a job. 'I hadn't long finished, maybe three years. Like some young ambitious footballers who end up retiring or giving up or dropping off panels, all you want to do is get coaching because you think that you would be good at it. Sometimes people like that think they would be better coaches than players. I wasn't thinking of the Dublin job, to be honest with you. It hadn't really occurred to me. I was still playing club football and enjoying it.'

In the Parnell Park dressing room, Whelan announced his resignation. One Dublin player got up to thank the departing boss, but the speech was delivered without much feeling. Many in the squad were indifferent, glad even. Whelan was done, and none of the players who hadn't responded to him during his two seasons in charge were going to start responding now.

The player's speech didn't sit well with some of the younger guys. One of those young players says: 'I didn't like it at all. For one of your own, whether you got on with him or not, for me as a young lad I didn't like it.' The behaviour of some sections of the supporters was also a bit of a shock. 'Here was a man who brought you in, and he resigned after two league games. That hadn't happened to a Dublin manager before. For a man who had won titles with Dublin, of a huge calibre, fans booing as he walked off – that was hard to take.'

'Players need to take responsibility because it works both ways. If things are not going well it's easy to blame the manager – but hold on a second, there's a difference between giving your all and not. Some weren't giving their all.' Carr, oblivious to Whelan's final moments, might have done with being a fly on the wall.

'Whelan didn't deserve it,' says Heery, who felt a huge loyalty towards his clubmate. 'That just shows you the muppets that follow Dublin, you know? There's a great core of Dublin GAA people, then there's the shower of muppets that go for the occasion. I don't go to big games now because I don't like listening to dickheads with five or six pints on board roaring at a fella while not having an idea about the effort in everything they've done. Slagging them.

'The players didn't give a damn, they were glad Mickey was gone. I felt very sorry for him. He had a great football brain.'

Heery doesn't hold a huge amount of affection for St Vincent's. 'I was a nobody in Vincent's compared to the main men who went before. You're kind of kept down like that. It took me a while to break into the team, and Mickey was the guy who gave me my first go. He and (ex-Dublin boss) Gerry McCaul gave me a go more so than Vincent's ever did and I respect those guys hugely. It's a hard-learning ground, that place.'

Johnny Magee reckons some players let Whelan down. He said: 'The players were lucky enough to play for Dublin so long, and looking back the responsibility is with them. My view was, it doesn't make a difference who the manager is, you should give 110 per cent every time. Should we have beaten Sligo? For sure.

'You go down the country and teams want to put it up to the Dubs. Any time you went out playing with Dublin there was always opposition would raise their game, you'd always see that. The belts would be harder. Some might say that's bollox but it's not bollox. I got used to that from a young age, under-12 Dublin all the way through – you find out going away from home the referee is against you, the umpire is against you. You got fucking nothing and had to fight your corner. I served my apprenticeship underage coming through. I knew it would be tough but you had to bide your time. It's hard to say if lads weren't giving their all but I felt we could have beaten both of those teams. Whether some lads were being half-arsed because of Mickey I don't know.'

Whelan lost it, according to Barr, in the delivery of his message. 'It may have been the case that fellas didn't buy into the trainer, rather than the training,' he says. For Magee, it was simply a fact that players so used to doing it one way couldn't see the value in another way, even if it was more effective.

County board Chairman John Bailey had pinned his hopes on Whelan. 'He was the mastermind technician behind Kevin Heffernan and the Dublin teams of the '70s and '80s,' Bailey says. 'He was a phenomenal brain, and with all his problems and errors he was a phenomenal coach. Some of the older gang didn't like Mickey or his ways and techniques.'

As usual, the process of finding a new manager was not all plain sailing. In November, clubs had put forward a number of candidates, but they were ignored in favour of a management committee established to select the right man. Tommy Lyons was once more in the frame, as was Dom Twomey, who had coached the Kilmacud Crokes, All-Ireland winners under Lyons in 1995. But the board's committee took a punt on Tommy Carr, a huge fans' favourite.

Carr was appointed on a three-year contract. But Gerry Brady, a member of the committee, told delegates that Carr had already agreed to stand down if at any point things went badly. John O'Leary was Carr's right-hand man, with Richie Crean and Twomey completing the set-up.

When news of the appointment broke, some of the players who had played for so long with Carr were doubtful. They viewed him with an uncomfortable mix of historical allegiance, respect, friendship, indifference and mild bewilderment. Carr was known during his playing days by some colleagues as 'GiveMeTheBall' because he was seen to be a man who wanted everything channelled through him. They weren't sure they saw him as a manager they wanted to play under.

The new boss faced a few immediate problems. How to get more from players who had fallen over the line two years earlier, yet were still playing? How to dispose of legends who were no longer at the races? How close could he be to the lads he had played with before? Could he be as ruthless and unforgiving as the mentors in his professional career, or would he have to adopt a softer approach?

Carr was a Captain in the Defence Forces, a veteran of tours in the Lebanon and Israel. He had a reputation for being no-nonsense and a bit stuffy. At the time, he felt his experience with soldiers in the army was all the preparation he needed to manage Dublin. 'I was an army officer, I had dealt with people all along. It's not as if I needed training in dealing with people. I had been in an authoritative position, out to the Lebanon and back. I had done all that sort of thing, so from my point of view I didn't see that as being an issue.'

But Dublin had a dressing room full of big personalities. Keith Barr, Dessie Farrell and Paul Curran were not going to accept being barked at by a guy they knew so well.

The new manager didn't have a managerial style yet, so he would have to borrow an MO from his playing days, when the way to succeed was to work, and then work some more. He says now: 'I got on very well with all the players, maybe to the degree ultimately I wasn't hard enough on them. I was so conscious of being an army officer and trying to not be like I was an officer in the changing room. You try to play it down a bit rather than use it – which, yes, might have been an inexperience thing from going into football management too early.

'I was trained to take a company of 130 men into a war zone, so of course I'm going to be able to manage a football team. But it's a different management set-up. If I go into the Lebanon with 130 guys I say, "Right, I want ten there, ten there, shut the fuck up, get it done, see you in the morning" – and you don't want to be like that. So maybe you come back a bit too much. Jim Gavin is an army officer, he's probably more dictatorial now than I was then. Brian Cody is more dictatorial than Jim, so you can make up any excuses you want, but at the end of the day unless you have the body of players willing to do what's necessary, it doesn't really matter.'

Keith Barr and his former half-back-line colleague had a mutual disdain for one another, united only in their love for the jersey. They had played together for so long. Too long. Barr didn't relish the prospect of having to take orders from his former colleague. But he'd get on with it, for Dublin's sake.

Barr was tough, an uncompromising and sometimes brutal competitor. For all his physical battles over a decade in blue, colleagues can recall perhaps one time when he got in over his head. It was against Armagh. Could have been league, could have been a friendly. Things were getting heated as they tended to do, and Barr took a swing at one of the Grimley brothers. Both Mark and John were 6' 2" and weighed almost 16 stone. Whichever one he tried to knock over stood firm, a mighty oak refusing to fall. All Barr could do to save himself a hiding was to hug him. He survived.

Carr, too, was unyielding and ultra-competitive – and Barr knew it. 'I played a lot of football with him, but there was one thing I wouldn't take growing up with Tommy and that was him being a dictator. We clashed many times because I wouldn't buy in to his dictatorship. I believe Tommy bought into his army credentials, that "because I'm an officer I'm the natural leader of men". But I can tell you this, if Tommy Carr was my officer and we went to war, we'd all be fucking dead. That's it.'

Despite the unhealthy dynamic between the two, Barr had respect for Carr: 'Tommy always had to work hard at what he done. He was strong, he was dogged, he would genuinely die for you. When he went out on the field, and no more than myself, when we crossed the white line there was only one thing that drew us all together, and that was Dublin. We didn't have to sleep, eat and drink in one another's company, but once we crossed that line I would put my life on the block for Tommy Carr and I genuinely would expect he would do the same. And I know he did.'

Barr faced into 1998 with his old foe calling the shots, and he knew early on that he was one of the players Carr wanted rid of. He reckoned it was his influence in the dressing room and his seniority in the Dublin ranks, rather than his waning powers of play, that had him marked out. 'I wasn't old then. I always felt Tommy wanted rid of me because I was a threat to him. Because I would question him at meetings.'

Carr agonized over whether to employ the carrot or the stick to fire up his weary charges. He offered trials to some long-serving players. One of these was Paul Clarke, the same fella who had been labouring since '95 to prove to Whelan that he wasn't a busted flush. This was Carr's way of testing Clarkie's desire, a commodity the Whitehall Colmcille man possessed in spades.

'I got a call to say there was a trial match tomorrow, on a Saturday,' says Clarke, who worked in the Airport Police Fire Rescue Service. 'I told him I was working, to leave it with me, I'll do my best to get off. Short notice for shift work in the airport isn't easy. I'd always plan weeks in advance, organizing my swaps so I could play and train. So I tried to swap, to no avail, couldn't go sick, I had no holidays left, so I said, "Look, I can't get off tomorrow, let me know when the next one is and we'll take it from there." But I never really heard anything after that.' (Carr, for his part, recalls that a small number of experienced players felt they shouldn't have had to prove themselves in a trial, though he doesn't name Clarke.)

Clarke is adamant that he wasn't offended at being asked to try out for a team he had represented for more than a decade. He said: 'It wouldn't make a difference, I'm competitive anyway, you could say, well I'm above that, but I'm not. Each year is a new year, each year a different challenge, one manager goes, another comes in, I always got on well with Carr and O'Leary, they know my strengths. If I've to go out and compete, I feel I'm a good footballer, I'll go out and prove I'm a good footballer. I like a challenge, you know?'

The incident was a microcosm of the uncertainty prevailing at the time. Carr spent his first six months on the job working largely with what he had. 'I never had a problem having to make hard calls or drop fellas even though my first inclination was to work with whatever was there. I really wanted to turn it around with the remnants of that All-Ireland-winning team because there were still a lot of them around. Now, in hindsight, I'd gone into management a bit too early after finishing playing, dealing with too many guys I'd been playing with. I could look back and say that now. Would it have been any different if there was ten years in it? Maybe it would, maybe it wouldn't, God only knows. If you look back at the nature of teams when they win an All-Ireland like that, there's always a dip unless they're being followed – like the current Dublin team – with plenty of players coming off the conveyor belt.

'That team I took over was maxed – in fact it maxed, I'd say, when I was on it in 1992, '93 and '94, when we should have won All-Irelands and didn't. They'll kill me for saying it but that [1995] team fell over the line. Let's call a spade a spade: they fell over the line and were lucky in 1995. So you could look back now and say there was no more in that team, they had maxed out. But it's easier said than done to get rid of players.'

Some of the players who came along after 1995 paint a bleak picture of the dressing room at the time, one bitterly divided between the All-Ireland winners and the rest; by club loyalties; and even by whether players were from the Northside or the Southside.

'Tommy was a peculiar beast,' says one player from that time. 'While he was from Dublin, he wasn't really from Dublin because he was half Tipperary, a culchie. That was highly unusual in Dublin football at the time when you either were a Dub or you weren't. The lads used to slag him behind his back because he was the army man who was super fit. Tommy wasn't in that 1995 clique but he wanted to be in it. The Currans and Barrs, they weren't all that fond of him I don't think, but when he came in as manager they kind of manipulated him to suit themselves. John O'Leary had a big say in everything that went on. He had a big connection with a lot of lads on the panel. O'Leary didn't want to let go, because this was their lives, how could he let go? But some believe it was to the detriment of the squad.'

Heery was happy to row in behind his former teammate – despite his heritage. 'Tommy is from Tipperary. But I never had a problem with that, I'd fucking say it to him,' he says. 'But if you went to battle with Tommy Carr you went to battle, and he wouldn't fucking let you down. So, I had no issues. Tommy could be very stern, but that was required.'

While Carr was deliberating over his managerial blueprint, newcomers rarely enjoyed the arm-around-the-shoulder treatment. Mick O'Keeffe was a star with the all-conquering Kilmacud Crokes but found it difficult to get a prolonged run in the Dublin team until the '99 league campaign. The corner forward pointed to O'Leary as an example of how not to motivate players. 'One day in training I was kicking a few frees. My confidence was up after kicking eight points against Mayo in a challenge, a few days before. O'Leary came

up to me and says, "You can't kick frees from the bench."'
O'Keeffe laughs about it now.

As a player, Carr had been introduced to the Dublin senior ranks in the 1985 Leinster championship by Heffernan,
who used to provoke frenzied debates with his players during team meetings. The searing introspection was often
survival-of-the-fittest stuff. Carr survived, won an All-Star
in 1991 and nearly won an All-Ireland, more than once.

'My first experience was with Kevin, who was no nonsense too,' he says. 'If I criticize a player now it's nearly,
"Fuck, you'll hurt his feelings and his confidence will be
shot," but in those days it wasn't like that. I remember Pat
O'Neill coming to me after one of the drawn games against
Meath in 1991 and saying, "Tom, you got a roasting off
Tommy Dowd." I said "Yeah, I did, Pat." He said, "That's
not going to happen again, sure it's not Tom?" I said, "It's
not, Pat." And that was fucking it. In other words, you fucked
up last Sunday, what are you going to do about it? I did grand
the next day. There was no "Don't worry about it, relax."

'You either do it or you don't – and Heffernan was the very
same, he'd tell you you didn't play well, you were shite on
Sunday. I remember one of the first meetings with Heffernan, I was a young fella in awe of all these guys in the Dublin
team who had won so much. He said, "Tom, how do you
think Kieran Duff played on Sunday?" I was silent, so he
said, "Come on, how do you think he played?" I said he
could have maybe passed the ball there. He said "You're dead
right. Did you hear that, Kieran? Any more of that fucking
around and you're gone out of here." That's it, that's your
coaxing and your cajoling. You either did it or you didn't.
And if you feel bad about it, tough, you get on with it.

'I didn't think that would work in 1998, with the Keith

Barrs of this world. I said, "Look, lads, I know I played with ye, let's come on, we can make this." I nearly became – I won't say I became a player again, I didn't, I kept that distance as much as I could, but it was a case of "Come on, lads, let's give it one more fucking lash here. What's in ye, let's give it a go." And they bought into it to a large degree, in fairness to them, but it just wasn't there, that visceral feeling of winning wasn't there any more.'

Under Robbie Kelleher, the 1970s stalwart who had taken over from Tommy Lyons, Kilmacud Crokes was blazing a trail on the fiercely contested club-scene. Their emergence was a source of displeasure to some on the panel, previously dominated by traditional 'Dub' clubs – Ballymun Kickhams, Erin's Isle, Na Fianna and St Vincent's. Crokes were seen in some quarters as posh, or even culchie.

It seems petty now, but the feeling festered, back in 1998. Mick O'Keeffe is convinced the bitter rivalries on the club scene spilled over into the county set-up. He said: 'We were spectacular at club level that year, kicking teams off the pitch. It was Tommy's first full year in charge, so me and Cossie [Ray Cosgrove] got in, and Johnny Magee was on the panel already. In Crokes there was very much a thing that it was club first and county second. And I think people in Dublin resented that, and the Crokes lads always felt they didn't get a proper crack of the whip with Dublin. Loads of Crokes lads felt they weren't part of it and walked away from Dublin panels.

'I think there was a feeling in Dublin that Crokes lads weren't really Dublin lads. Robbie Leahy and Peter Ward didn't get a fair crack, and [sub goalkeeper] Mick Pender walked away because he couldn't get in. The first of ours to break into a Dublin championship squad consistently was

Johnny Magee, but Johnny was in with Curran and Barr and those fellas. They didn't really see Johnny as Kilmacud, if that makes sense – they thought he was a real Dub. Johnny would go out and thump the head off culchies, and they loved that. They didn't like the more thoughtful, soft Crokes lads,' he laughs.

Magee was the Crokes trailblazer. He was the player the rest looked up to, and he had that physical and mental edge the others were missing. He was raw in 1998, but he took no prisoners. Magee was exactly the type of player the survivors of '95 would welcome into a panel, Southsider or not. He says: 'I was close to some of the senior players at the time, and had no inhibitions, because I was trying to kick down a door to become a regular Dublin player. No Crokes player had been a regular in Dublin squads before me; some lads had been in and out but never regular. Stories would come back about what was done to the lads.

'I had been with Dublin all the way through underage, captained the minors in '96, so there was no fucking way I wasn't going to kick down that door. I started mingling with the senior lads, drinking with the likes of Deego [Mick Deegan] and Paul Bealin. Paddy Moran and Heery were very good to me, Curran would put the arm around the shoulder, Dessie too. They looked out for us at different stages, a bit of encouragement which I found was great. Was that because I was a cheeky pup? I didn't let their stature intimidate me. Yes I was in awe of them, I looked up to them, I had watched them from Hill 16, and then I found myself in that kind of company. I was in the dressing room, I was watching as a kid but wasn't afraid. I said, "I'm gonna show these legends what I'm made of." That was the way I went at it, and maybe that's why they took me in quicker. I didn't back down.

'I remember going toe to toe with Gavin, Stynesy and Barrsy, stood my ground, and gave as good as I got. I wouldn't back away, I would probably get a bit of a hiding but I was gonna go down swinging. I remember getting winded in a challenge match and Heery coming over, grabbing me by the scruff. I was winded but he said, "Don't let them fuckers see you're hurt. I don't care if your leg is falling off, you get up and you get on with it. Don't let those culchies see you hurt." I'll never forget it. And until the day I stopped putting a jersey on my back, there was no way I'd let them see me hurt.'

Magee had to be tough because Crokes players had a history of getting it in the neck. One Dublin panellist once had to fetch his sodden gear bag from the showers after one of the players put it in for a wash. Another was poolside with the squad on a holiday when one player began handing out cans, deliberately skipping the Kilmacud man. It was petty stuff, right out of playschool, but those stories filtered down.

Barr, no fan of softies, acknowledged the divide – but was adamant it didn't stem from him. 'I certainly would not resent Crokes players. But it's a very interesting question, as even today there's a Northside/Southside thing in Dublin football, of course there is. See the power in the county board. Where's the chairman from? Northside. Go over the history, how many from the Southside? Welcome to the politics of Dublin. Where's the head office? On the Northside. There always has been a north–south divide,' he says, adding with a grin as wide as the Liffey: 'Even in the supporters. A Northsider goes with his can of Bulmers and his quarter-pounder, hat and scarf and horse and cart. The Southsider goes in his Rolls Royce and his prawn sandwich.

'I didn't see them as softer, or less Dublin. There was no resentment from me. But I can understand why other people could say that because that divide was always spoken about. You can look at the teams over the years, the majority of the teams, players were all from the Northside,' Barr added.

For the manager, too, the divide was always there. 'That kind of Crokes/Ballymun/Vincent's thing was always there in Dublin football,' Carr says. 'Because Crokes were the country boys, they represented everything that was good and bad about the Southside; Ballymun and Vincent's and Erin's Isle represented everything that was good and bad about the Northside. You had that natural clash and they were probably clashing in club championships as well. But did I think it was big? Maybe I missed it, but it was not necessarily a massive thing – not so much that it divided the team. Maybe it went over my head?'

Meath legend Graham Geraghty, whose club Seneschalstown had played and been beaten by Crokes in Leinster competition, reckoned from the outside that Crokes were under-represented in a Dublin set-up that was crying out for fresh blood. 'The calibre wasn't there that was there before, as happens at some stage with every county. At that time, they didn't have lads who were interested in giving it everything for the county. There might have been better players playing club football than what they had at the time, which also happens in every county. Whether they didn't want to play or weren't selected, it's hard to put your finger on it. Dublin seemed to be going through a period where nothing was going right. Kilmacud won the All-Ireland and I'm not sure whether any Crokes player was on that team then.'

Many players felt Carr wasn't decisive enough to get to the root of the biggest problem: player power. One former player remembers the day of a league game in that era when a senior player who had been benched threatened to walk out unless he was selected. He started the game.

O'Keeffe, who is reluctant to criticize Carr, says: 'I think there was a huge amount of player power, and I think there were damaging cliques, and clubs not favoured by management for various reasons. People will say if they were good enough they'd have got in and there might be an element of that too. The cliques were fellas who played together for years, won All-Irelands and were getting into their thirties, and there was big club rivalries. People forget this too, Dublin players were released to play for their clubs all the time. You could have a league match involving Crokes and Erin's Isle – Keith Barr, Johnny Barr, Eddie Barr, Charlie Redmond, Mick Deegan, Robbie Boyle, Ken Spratt – all these guys playing for Isles on a small club pitch and on the other side seven or eight from Crokes on either county panels outside Dublin or on the fringes of the Dublin panel, and you would get seriously competitive matches, week in week out. You don't get that now at club level, which is a huge loss at club level but not maybe at county. But because that club rivalry existed it did spill over and you had big battles between lads. A bit like what you hear in other counties, I don't think the club rivalry was good for the county team.

'It spilled over into training. It spilled over into socializing too: lads travelled together in separate groups to training, to matches. There was a disconnect. You're travelling with your mates you played with week in week out, you're bitching about lads, you think you should be in ahead of guys from Na Fianna. You'd be saying they're only in ahead of you because their mate is captain and half a selector, that kind of thing. There's not much difference between fellas at that level, and some lad is getting picked ahead of you who's not as good as you are, so there was a feeling that there's politics at play. When you get older you do the same thing, you're talking yourself on to the team, in the manager's ear. I'm not throwing them under the bus, it's human nature: they don't want lads coming in.'

The team that would take to the field to play Kildare in Carr's first Leinster championship game as manager in the summer of 1998 contained Paddy Moran, Paul Curran, Keith Barr, Paul Bealin and Jim Gavin. Eamon Heery and Mick Deegan were on the bench. These players, though still willing to train ferociously, were living on borrowed time.

Carr knew he was in trouble. Panellists had come and gone during the league campaign, and few of them got him excited. Carr admits he made far more changes than he would have wanted, but for a reason: the players were crap. 'I'll tell you what I didn't have,' he says, almost twenty years of contemplation later. 'I won't name names, but I had a lot of average players. That's me saying it here now. One of the reasons I had ten guys going for corner forward position is because not one of them was sticking his hand up and saying, "I fucking want it more than anyone else." Does a manager want to be looking at ten guys? No, he doesn't. A manager wants to look at one guy for each position and say, "These are the best by a mile." If you're on a team and looking at seven fellas for a position, you're having a difficulty with that position.

'If you go to the established teams, they won't have that problem. You will name thirteen of the starting Dublin championship team. Bang, bang, bang, OK, lads, what do you think we should do with those two positions on Sunday? With the other teams you're discussing six or seven positions, that's the problem. I'd have loved the headache of having thirteen nailed-on starters.'

It was muttered, by some of the younger players, that the

senior guys who had played alongside Carr attempted to manipulate his selection decisions for the championship. There were rumours – convincingly denied by both men – that Keith Barr came out of a meeting with Carr in April of that season, claiming he knew the starting fifteen for the Kildare game.

Off the field, Carr was dealing with issues he could have done without. Earlier in the year, his captain, Dessie Farrell, had been charged with drink driving. The news did not make the papers – until the morning of the Kildare match. Farrell, whose marriage was breaking down at the time, later revealed in his autobiography that he had considered taking his own life. Carr backed him all the way, and that compassion helped Farrell emerge from his own darkness as well as forging a deeper relationship between the pair that would endure until Carr's final days as boss.

Carr retained Jim Gavin as free-taker as he completed his evolution from defensive wing forward to scorer-in-chief. Some of his teammates dubbed Gavin 'Champo Jim', in a dig at what they saw as favouritism towards the veteran. Carr, for his part, valued Gavin's attitude and leadership. 'Jim was one of those guys you could say, "Jim, you were shite on Sunday." And he'd say, "Yeah, I know that," and that would be it. There'd be no "What do you mean I was shite, sure didn't I score a point?" "You did, Jim, but you missed seventeen of them" – none of that. Jim would put his hands up, say, "Sorry, lads, I didn't do well on Sunday, it won't happen again." I saw leadership in Jim, I thought he'd keep things together up front. And we came from the same kind of background, in the army: we'd have been talking the same language.'

Gavin had been used during the '95 campaign as a defensive

wing forward. His job was to stop the marauding wing backs that were starting to become common in the game, but he disliked the role, and he scrapped with Pat O'Neill over it. It was a dirty job and someone had to do it, and it was a job Gavin got stuck into despite his misgivings, famously putting Graham Geraghty in his place during the Leinster final that year. But by the time Carr took over, Gavin wanted to be an out-and-out forward, and the new manager was happy to let him express himself.

Declan Darcy had made the move to Dublin from Leitrim, starting the Kildare game at full-forward, as he had throughout the National league. He was another big personality and someone the newcomers looked up to. He didn't carry the baggage of '95 but had a footballing pedigree, having won a Connacht title in 1994. As one recalled: 'Darcy was always of the view that the next young fella through the door could win you an All-Ireland. There was none of that jealously guarding his jersey, so he was respected.' He was set to play a key role, as a scoring forward in a squad not blessed with them.

Darcy found out early on what it meant to be a Dublin footballer in those days. During a day off on a weekend away, when the Dubs were scheduled to play Sligo on the Friday night and Roscommon on the Sunday, the newcomer was tempted away for a few pints with a couple of the established players. Come midnight, the three Dublin stars were in their last pub of the night. While Darcy popped out to the loo, one of the players arranged with the barman to start pouring them shots – only for every shot of booze for Darcy, the two other lads were to be given water. 'Declan ended up drinking a bottle of tequila. He fell out of the place, and the head on him the next day for the match was a sight to behold!'

laughed one of the drinkers years later. 'There's a big difference between drinking and playing for Leitrim and playing and drinking for the Dubs.'

Carr sprinkled the team with as much energy as he could. Brian Barnes from St Sylvester's was at corner back, Dermot Harrington from Naomh Mearnog on front of him at number 7. Paddy Christie at full back, Ian Robertson at number 12 and Ciaran Whelan at 10 were already established as players whom the new man hoped to build a team around. Shane Ryan, a colleague of Harrington's from Mearnog, was on a championship bench that summer for the first time. He says: 'I thought this was unbelievable! I even said to one of the lads on the way to training, "Oh my god, imagine if I'm even asked to warm up, I won't know what to do. I'll shit myself."'

Kildare were where Kildare usually are, close to a breakthrough. Manager Mick O'Dwyer had a strong spine of players, including Glenn Ryan, Niall Buckley, Davy Dalton and Declan Kerrigan, as well as Martin Lynch and the emerging Anthony Rainbow and Dermot Early. The previous summer had seen the Lilywhites take All-Ireland champions Meath to the wire in an epic three-game saga for the Leinster title.

Even on the first Championship Sunday, some of the Dublin players couldn't resist throwing their weight around with teammates. Magee, named on the subs bench for his first championship game in Croke Park, was reminded where he stood in the pecking order when he went to take his seat in the dressing room. 'Barrsy and Heery said to me, "Get the fucking boat, get your bag out of there. History was made on those seats",' he recalls, laughing. Magee moved over. His turn to decide where he sat on match day would come.

The game was dreadful to watch, finishing 0-10 to 0-10, with just eight scores from play in total. The dearth of scoring forwards in Dublin was obvious to the 60,058 people who paid in to see it. Jim Gavin's late equalizer was worth €500,000 to the Leinster Council, which did quite well out of replays in those days. Heery, named on the subs bench but itching for some action, got the fans excited at half-time. Magee recalls: 'Jogging out at half-time, Heery was coming out from underneath the Hogan with me, but when I turned around he was gone. He disappeared. I looked to me left and looked around, next thing I see him burying Martin Lynch a shoulder into the back, and running backwards, pointing at him, saying "I'm coming to get you!" It was brilliant, I'm looking at Lynch laughing. He was putting his marker down, it was hilarious.'

The couple of weeks between the drawn game and the replay presented a chance for some of those who didn't play the first day to stake their claim. It was also a chance for those who hadn't impressed to find ways of hanging on to the jersey, and for Carr to employ a technique he'd picked up from Heffo.

Barr recalls a training session in the days after the drawn game where he went head to head with the manager in front of the rest of the squad. 'I always remember we were over in a barracks after training and we did a video session of the drawn game,' he said. 'Tommy asked the young lads what they thought. Young lads, because they're young lads, won't rock the boat. I saw it as a leader picking on weak people. So at the end of the meeting, the video was turned off and he says, "Well, Keith, what do you think?" I said, "Tommy, put that video back on, and do you have an hour?" We sat through it again. And I questioned him on everything. He didn't like it. Welcome to hardened Dublin. I questioned him that night, the whole squad looking on. Nobody else said anything.

'I sat through that first screening for the best part of fifty minutes and I kept my mouth shut and never said anything. But it was him who asked me. And if I'm to be true to myself, and true to being a leader, and true to my fellow players, well I let him fucking have it. I couldn't care less that nobody else got involved. When I'm asked for my opinion, I don't give a shit whether you like it or not.'

For the replay, veterans Deegan and Heery were recalled at corner back and half back, an admission from Carr that his options were limited when it came to replacing the old warhorses. Midfielder Paul Bealin was benched, while Gavin moved to the 40. Despite a late goal from Darcy, Kildare won by 0-12 to 1-8. The Lilywhites hadn't beaten Dublin in championship football since 1972. O'Dwyer's troops went on to beat Meath in the Leinster final, and to reach their first All-Ireland final in fifty-three years, beating reigning champions Kerry in the semi-final. They were beaten 1-14 to 1-10 by a Pádraic Joyce-inspired Galway, the Tribesmen lifting Sam Maguire for the first time since 1966. Galway boss John O'Mahony could also boast Ja Fallon, Niall Finnegan and the majestic Michael Donnellan in a star-studded attack that showed Dublin just how far behind they had fallen.

Almost twenty years on, Keith Barr can barely contain his frustration when he recalls how tamely Dublin let their neighbours in. He had fought like a man possessed against the white tide in the early '90s and was sick when it finally engulfed his team. Barr slams his fist on the table, momentarily back in that dressing room, the bitter taste of defeat lingering in his mouth. 'That was the first time Kildare had beaten us in championship football in decades. If you know anything about elite sport, you don't give your opposition an inch. And what happened to Kildare that year? They got to an All-Ireland final. Then they got to two. See what I mean?

'We knew, if someone comes up and beats you, you're giving them self-belief. You're giving them confidence. You've opened the door. The light is there for them, and when there's light down the tunnel, players will follow it. When you're in a dark room you don't know where the fuck you're going.'

3. Dogs and Prostitutes

Following the defeat to Kildare, Carr still wasn't ready to give up on 1998. Dublin embarked on a series of challenge games against teams still remaining in the championship. He took his troops, shorn of some of the '95 stalwarts but reinforced by eager newcomers, around the country to see what he had at his disposal. It wasn't what he had in mind when he took the job, but it was all he could do to begin planning for the 1999 Leinster championship.

'I remember going to Derry, where we started to build a nucleus,' Carr says. 'We were like prostitutes looking for trial games, and it started from there. Only the lads who really wanted to be there were there. Fellas who'd come up to Derry on a Saturday afternoon in August or September to play a challenge game. There weren't a whole lot of the '95 players involved.'

Paddy Christie, Ciaran Whelan and Ian Robertson were the type of player any manager could build a team around. Carr started to run the rule too over minors, including Manus Breathnach, Declan Conlon, former ball boy and '95 squad favourite Wayne McCarthy and Collie Moran, a highly rated youngster from Ballyboden St Enda's with no senior experience even at club level. Moran knew from the first day he walked in that Dublin's wasn't a particularly happy camp.

Punishing sessions in the Phoenix Park were designed to bring fitness levels back up to the required standard. Moran was in awe at the roll call. Dessie, Curran, Gavin and Stynes were players he had long admired; the likes of Whelan, Robertson and Christie the ones he wanted to emulate.

The championship draw in November was to them like Christmas. 'Leinster was a very different landscape at the time, it was before the back door so it was do or die,' says Moran. 'Not many people pay attention now for the draw when it's made in November for the following summer, but back then it was a huge deal. We were looking at the draw, if Meath and Kildare were on the other side we were thinking we've a great chance of getting to a Leinster final. If you won that you were straight through to an All-Ireland semi-final.'

Carr had been given a free pass in 1998, but in Dublin one season of mediocrity in league and championship was enough. The following year would have to bring about an improvement. Carr needed characters.

One player he was desperate to keep was Paddy Moran, an unheralded corner back who went about his business quietly and effectively. If you were to rank all the 1995 names by star quality, Moran's was close to the bottom. But within the Dubs' set-up, everyone knew the worth of the Whitehall Colmcille man. In club football, special regard is reserved for the tough old boys from the north county. The Dubs needed a few of those. Carr says: 'I remember having discussions with John O'Leary and he said, "Tom, we need to go out the north side and get some dogs, some Mick Kennedys from the Ward. Real dogs." And he was right. But we didn't find any dogs. And the dog that we had, Paddy Moran, I was disappointed to lose him. Even though he was thirty-one or thirty-two at the time and he came and said, "Tom, I can't do this any more, my fucking knee is killing me," I tried to convince him to stay another year. And Paddy wasn't the best player in the world now, but he was a fucking dog. He was one of the reasons Dublin won an All-Ireland. The least talented player, but one of the reasons they won in '95.'

They began training early. And hard. Players remember a brutal, punishing regime to get them up to a standard of fitness that was by now becoming commonplace in teams around the country. Magee recalls: 'I wasn't part of plans from the beginning. I had to fight my way in. It was a difficult time. I broke my bollocks, trained hard, saw more of the lads than my family, as Tommy felt we weren't as fit as we could have been. We trained Monday, Wednesday, Friday and Sunday for the guts of two or three months, during the league. It was a tough fucking shift. Cathal Brugha Barracks and the Magazine Fort, around the fucking cross in the park, I'll never forget it. He felt we had to do it.'

It paid off, with Dublin enjoying their first decent league campaign in years. They emerged from Group A, third behind Armagh and Cork. With three wins, two draws and two defeats – and just four goals altogether – it wasn't all plain sailing. But it was progress.

The squad was exhausted. Players would at times have to drag themselves into their cars following yet another pitiless night in the Rathmines barracks, minds clouded with the thought of coming back in two days' time to do it all over again. Athletes in the prime of their playing lives at times struggled to walk as Carr's trainers closed out punishing sessions not necessarily designed for Gaelic footballers. The sessions got them fit, but few of them were improving as players. It was often a struggle to keep the eyes focused on the road as they drove home. For all the sprinting up hills, so few of them could kick a ball over the bar.

The 1998/9 national league campaign was notable for the fact that many teams – recognizing the need to step up the demands of training – appeared to be happy to bow out of the competition relatively early. In April, Dublin gained a semblance of revenge when overcoming Kildare in the national league quarter-final, then overcame Armagh in a replay to reach the final against Cork in Pairc Uí Chaoimh. It was a miserable day for the abject Dubs, just 3,000 fans there to witness the 0-12 to 1-7 defeat.

As the summer approached, change was afoot in the GAA. The Football Development Committee was discussing the need for alterations in the structure of the football championships. They discussed round robin or two-tiered championships, and even contemplated eliminating the national league. Even allowing for the indifference of the Cork public to the league, the attendance of 3,000 for a final involving the Dubs was pathetic and a source of huge alarm. Everyone knew that teams needed more summer football, but the FDC were battling against a congress deeply set in its ways, and nobody seemed to have a solution. For now, the status quo would have to do. Dublin and everyone else would have to continue playing, knowing one championship defeat meant curtains.

Dublin's league run masked a few problems approaching championship time – including a lingering division between older and younger players. Mick O'Keeffe recalls: 'There were players who had an influence in team selection, some of the senior players with big personalities and glorious CVs who were quite vocal about how things should be done. Maybe having player-driven teams is important, but it went too far sometimes. It didn't help young lads trying to break in to the panel, there was a split between the emerging players such as Ian Robertson and the more established players. There were punch-ups during training matches. There was bad blood.

'Tommy tried a few times to get things out in the open. One day there was an open forum where stuff was said. Sometimes that's good, sometimes bad. You hear about the Irish rugby lads in Carton House, Leinster and Munster together, they all got it off their chests, things that were bugging fellas, and it cleared the air. But this was vicious, stuff was aired that probably shouldn't have been said. They ended up calling it the St Valentine's Day Massacre. Robertson was a bright guy, he would have said his piece and a few of the older fellas said things, and that ends up spilling over on to training pitches.'

Another problem was what to do about Keith Barr. The Erin's Isle man remained an idol on Hill 16, but the 1998/9 league campaign was the end of the road for his Dublin career, which had spanned a decade in the senior ranks. He was thirty years old.

He insists with his customary grin that the manner of his departure doesn't rankle, but the emotion in his voice betrays his words. 'Tommy was weak and I believe his biggest mistake was when he did his best to get rid of me. I didn't retire from Dublin football. I wasn't told I wasn't wanted. I can't honestly remember how it ended, maybe a squad was picked and I wasn't on it. Nobody picked up the phone to me, nobody put the arm around the shoulder. Nobody thanked me for A, B and C. Did I look for any of it? No, I didn't. Thank you very much. No final farewell, and I didn't want one either.'

Barr's son was born that year, adding to his young family, and he was busy with work. The children kept him sane, in case his inner strength betrayed him. Weak moments are for weak people. Block them out.

Carr says: 'Is it difficult to tell Keith Barr he's not playing?

Yeah. We had the discussions. Was it difficult? Yes, it was. Did I get stick? Yes, I did. These were guys I had played with. From a public-perception point of view you're dropping household names and that's not what anyone sets out to do. You'd prefer to make your name out of getting the best out of household players and being remembered as somebody who really fucking rejuvenated Keith Barr. You'd like it if people said, "He really got Paul Clarke going again." Nobody goes out to make a name out of a negative situation.'

The question of loyalty doesn't arise in Barr's mind. 'Tommy getting rid of me wasn't disloyal – because I never had a relationship with him. You're only let down by close friends and family, or yourself.'

At the same time, Barr sees the big picture: players come and players go. 'One has to understand, what makes a team? We had army officers, firemen, ambulance men, doctors. We had students, labourers, brickies, carpenters, teachers, bank managers, and you throw them into a fucking pot. These people came from Killiney, Dalkey, Stillorgan, Darndale, Coolock, Finglas, Ballymun. You're taking all these players from different backgrounds, education, upbringing, society, and you're moulding them into a team.

'We don't have time, lads, we simply don't have time. Don't put your arm around my shoulder. Because there ain't no back door. Do you understand? There ain't no back door.'

Dublin's frailties at centre half back had been exposed against Armagh, and Magee felt he deserved a crack at the shirt Barr had worn with distinction for a decade. Dublin were scheduled to play Louth in the first round as part of a double header also involving Meath and Wicklow. Robertson, the heir apparent at number 6 where Paul Curran had been for the league final, was surprisingly lumped in at full forward. Shane Ryan pushed up from the edge of the square to centre back, where Magee wanted to be. Dublin won easily against abysmal opponents, but the knives were being sharpened, just in case. The absence of Barr and Paul Bealin was a source of annoyance to fans, some of whom were waiting for a bad performance to reinforce their point.

Up the other end of the pitch, Mick O'Keeffe still wasn't having much joy. He remembers: 'In the league final against Cork I came on as a sub with fifteen minutes to go when we were never going to win the match. He emptied the bench, we got a goal, and they were much better than us. It was in the lashings of rain, every time I played it seemed to rain. And I played into the wind!

'I'm not saying I should have played but I definitely felt there was a bit of maybe I was from the wrong club, my face didn't fit, all that kind of stuff. As a young lad what you need is a consistent run of matches, a manager who tells you you're great. In fairness to management they're going to look at Meath in the championship and say, "Am I going to pick that lad from Crokes who I'm sixty per cent sure of or am I going to pick Jim Gavin who's won an All-Ireland and I'm eighty per cent sure of? OK, so maybe he's a bit past it, but I'm not going to risk this young fella, he could blow up his first big game in Croke Park and have a fucking meltdown. If there was a back door scenario you might have got more game time, but as it was lads wouldn't get a consistent run.'

Dublin's team for the Leinster semi-final against Laois was significantly different from the side that limped out the previous year to Kildare. In defence, Deegan, Barr and Heery had given way to Paul Croft, Tommo Lynch and Keith Galvin. Dermot Harrington was axed, and Jason Sherlock was named as a sub. Six All-Ireland winners remained in the starting XV, and the bench had a fresher feel with Senan Connell, O'Keeffe, Shane Ryan and Peadar Andrews all on board. On 27 June in front of only 28,371 fans, the Dubs escaped with a draw. Dublin had raced into a 6-point lead early on, but they were 4 down with three minutes to go, and were saved only by the inspired intervention of Robertson, with a goal and a 71st-minute fisted point. Laois goalkeeper Fergal Byron remembers that last point as somewhat dubious. 'Robertson picked the ball up off the ground. That's the first thing that comes into my mind,' Byron says.

With Dublin still struggling in attack, Sherlock was sprung back into action for the replay. And, following a chat with the manager, Johnny Magee finally got his chance to emerge from the shadows, named at centre back.

'Against Armagh and Cork in the league and Louth I was sitting on the bench, not getting a look-in. Then Laois came around, I didn't start so I had a pain in my hole at this stage. I went to Tommy after the drawn game, there was a two-week break, spoke with Dom [Twomey] first, then told Tommy I could do a job at centre back. I told him I won a club championship at centre back, [if he] put me in I wouldn't let him down. So what happened? He starts me against Laois. I went in and did well on Michael Lawlor, who was Man of the Match the first day. I didn't look back after that.'

Dublin won that replay, withstanding a late rally from Laois – who were down to 13 men.

The 1999 Leinster final between Dublin and Meath is remembered in the capital for the roasting Peadar Andrews received from Ollie Murphy. The St Brigid's man had been brought in at corner back for Lynch in the only change to the side from the Laois replay. But another decision taken by Carr was the one that rankled with the players, and events on the pitch added fuel to claims that the manager wasn't entirely in control.

Carr introduced Ray Cosgrove as a substitute, only to take him off 25 minutes later. It was a decision that prompted Cossie to walk away and stay away for two years. In the view of some of the other players, the humiliation could have wrecked his career. The forward, another from the growing stable of Kilmacud players, is still unhappy with it so many years later and he blames current Dublin boss Gavin for his miserable afternoon.

He says: 'I was told to go in at centre forward for Dessie. Jim [Gavin] was corner forward. He told me to switch, I fucked off as only a young fella would. Jim came out, I went in to the corner, no ball came in, and 25 minutes later I'm getting the shepherd's hook. I was a young kid at that stage, very green, and didn't have the balls to say, "Go fuck yourself, this is my position." I wasn't vocal or mean enough to say that then.

'It was a Leinster final, I should have come out and said, "No, I'm coming out to win my own ball. [Gavin] felt it was the right thing to do, the game was slipping away from us, to come out and win the ball. That's the short and the long of it. Tommy Carr was still struggling at that point. He didn't drop many seasoned guys, or make any big statement like that. I was deeply disappointed after being taken off and when he rang me to come back I said, "No thanks, I can't look you in the white of the eyes and give you any respect." He told me to go back to the club and he'd come look at me again and I said, "Tommy, I can't." I wasn't coming back.'

Murphy hit 1-5 and Trevor Giles 5 points in an emphatic 1-14 to 0-12 Meath win in front of 56,315. For Dublin, old-timers Darcy and Gavin grabbed 11 points between them, but it was nowhere near enough to topple a team who would go on to claim the All-Ireland title for the fourth time under Sean Boylan. Afterwards, Carr's tactics were questioned. Dangerman Giles had been given the freedom of Croke Park and, armed with all the time he needed, launched the type of ball in to Murphy that corner forwards thrive on.

For Meath, it was becoming all too easy. Following the drubbing in 1995, by this point the Royals were firmly in control against their hated rivals. Graham Geraghty knew that by 1999 they were in control. He said: 'I used to love playing them. Even going back to the '80s watching games, you always knew you'd be up against it. But by 1999 we were confident in our own ability and didn't fear Dublin. It was easier going out against them, you knew that psychologically you had the upper hand.'

Magee was alone among the Crokes contingent who felt he received at least a crack at the whip that summer. Other Crokes players in the set-up feel they were marginalized by management. Their clubmate Mick Pender had had a some-times unhappy spell as sub keeper with the Dubs, and the Crokes men wondered if this was somehow held against all of them.

Perennial substitute O'Keeffe didn't even make the bench this time. When that happens, thoughts sometimes run through a man's head that he doesn't recognize as his own. 'That day versus Meath, when you know you're not in the plans – this is terrible to say but you kind of hope the thing ends. I hate saying it, I really do.'

4. Mayhem

The 1999/2000 national league campaign represented a return to form for Dublin: they failed to qualify for the knock-out stages. But they didn't play all that badly. They were beaten only twice, away to Tyrone and Roscommon, overcoming Kerry, Armagh and Cork at home. They also dug in to record an impressive 2-15 to 0-20 win over 1998 All-Ireland champions Galway in what was a rare away win over one of the stronger counties. They conceded just three goals in their seven fixtures. The spine of Christie, Magee, Whelan, Farrell and Robertson was supported by old-timer Curran, Shane Ryan and Peadar Andrews in defence, and Collie Moran and Senan Connell in attack. Curran was by now the longest serving player on the panel, and in no mood to give up his number 5 shirt easily.

Dublin's early 2000 championship form was quietly impressive. Wexford were dispatched easily, as was par for the course in those days. Wexford forward John Hegarty recalls the mindset of a team coming to Croke Park with no realistic hope. 'You still have to prepare properly and convince yourself,' he says. 'I remember going on the bus, knowing in my heart of hearts we're not going to do it. Yet you still have your pasta, you still hydrate, and you wonder why you do it. Wexford fans will go up Saturday night, have a feed of pints in Coppers, have a burger, pull a bird if they can, go to Quinn's the next day for more pints, come into the stadium, and if things are going bad after ten minutes they'll say, "Ah for fuck's sake why did I bother coming up here wasting my time?"'

Once All-Ireland champions Meath exited in the quarter-final at the hands of Offaly, everyone expected a provincial decider between the Dubs and Kildare – and the pundits fancied Kildare. But the Lilies struggled against Louth and Offaly, and Mick O'Dwyer couldn't settle on his preferred team. Dublin had a chance.

On 30 July Kildare and Dublin played out a pulsating 14-point draw. The standard of fare served up in the Leinster championship had been dire, but this was on a different planet. This time it was Lilies forward Tadhg Fennin who did his bit for the council's coffers, missing a late chance to nick it for Kildare. Brian Stynes had his best game in a distinguished career, dragging his team back into it following an early Kildare blitz. Sherlock was moved to the 40 in the second half and orchestrated a three-point salvo in the opening six minutes. 50,066 watched the lead change hands a few times before Moran, a lad with little senior experience, rifled over a late equalizer. A Kildare winner would have been harsh.

Few remember that game. But nobody who was there two weeks later to witness the replay will ever forget it. At half-time, Dublin were champions. By the end, the dramatic extent of their decline was etched into the Croke Park concrete. To the watching world, Carr's men were finished, pure and simple.

Carr recalls: 'I was in the changing room at half-time. We were 6 points up and looking like we were going to win by 20. I remember one man, I won't name him, he said to me going out, "Tom, enjoy your Leinster title now."

'He was being genuine, he said, "You worked for this moment, you fucking enjoy it."'

Within two minutes of the restart the sides were level, and

a little over thirty-five minutes later, Dublin were out of the championship. Two goals in the space of a minute shortly after half-time knocked the stuffing out of a Dublin team no longer in the habit of winning big games in Croke Park. It was the most spectacular capitulation yet by the Dubs. The supporters stood in stunned silence on Hill 16, incapable of processing what they had just witnessed.

Shane Ryan remembers: 'It was a sickener. The year was great, we'd a decent league campaign, there was a buzz, things were going well, and going really well in the first half. When you think back, Kildare had a lot of strong players. They sucker-punched us in the second half and I remember a whole load of stories came out afterwards. At the time I remember thinking, "What are these people saying!" I was sick enough, but you'd still kind of laugh when you'd hear people say on the radio, "I know for a fact there was a big bust up in the dressing room at half-time," and I'd be thinking, "Hang on, I was in the dressing room! There was no bust up!" Where do these stories come from? I remember some fella ring in saying, "I'm the bus driver who drives the team everywhere and I can tell you for a fact John O'Leary runs the show there." "What?! Who is this guy? We know our bus driver. That's not him!"'

Carr, unsurprisingly, took a lot of flak, but Magee says: 'We let him down. It wasn't Tommy's fault: players went missing. Two goals in a minute, you're looking for fucking characters and leaders. You are looking for fellas to stand up. It wasn't Tommy's fault that day, it was the players' fault. We should have won the fucking thing. We did everything he asked us to do in the first half and then he told us to just do it again in the second and build on it. Then the two goals, fellas disappearing, lads didn't respond.'

That Dublin squad was beginning to develop a tight bond, finally casting off the shackles of '95. The players grew closer, and a drinking culture developed. Two-day sessions after games were not uncommon, and everyone was welcome. Only a handful, the teetotal Paddy Christie included, passed up the opportunity to go on the razz, whether they were getting a game or not.

Mick O'Keeffe recalls: 'There was a training-hard-but-drinking-hard culture among some of the lads. In the summertime, there was a thing with the old-school lads that you'd go hard at it over the Christmas, as the league was the league. But the Currans and Dessies, when May came, they were professionals. Dessie was an animal. He was a hard bastard, trained like mad.

'The drinkers were me and Johnny, some [other] lads would come and go, Darcy and Jim, Curran, some of the Ballymun lads, and it would splinter as the night goes on. Lads drank in different places. The Sunnybank was one, up Hanlon's corner, drinking around Stoneybatter, McGowan's, and end up in Coppers eventually. It was mainly the northside crew but I was involved. I'd drink with anyone. I would have been pally with Senan or Tommo Lynch from Na Fianna who our club had a huge rivalry with at the time so you'd have proper run-ins with them as well. [We were] out after every league game.

'There'd be a big blowout after championship matches. They're funny, you're off the jar for weeks and it's pent up so you go out and you might be out for two days then. They were proper sessions. You get disengaged from the panel, so you go on the piss the Friday before the Leinster final. Panel members would have done it. They would have togged on a Sunday but they knew they weren't within an arse's roar of the thing. So at that stage you're totally disengaged so you'll do whatever.'

Dublin's fifth place in Division 1A behind Galway, Roscommon, Tyrone and Offaly in 2000/2001 made for another forgettable National League campaign. Kerry finished second from bottom in the group, which once more saw most of the top teams prioritize experimentation over results. Carr's eyes, certainly, were on Leinster. Carr gave opportunities to the likes of Darren Homan in midfield, Enda Sheehy on the 40, and Wayne McCarthy, who had assumed free-taking responsibilities. Alan Brogan made his league debut in the opening defeat to Tyrone.

Mick O'Keeffe had been flying back to Dublin to play club games from his base in Brussels, where he was on a scholarship. For a man of learning, he fell into the old trap of judging a book by its cover. It happened in a league match against Kerry: 'I remember walking down towards corner forward, there's this corner forward's trick you'd try and suss out the ropey corner back. I saw Mike Hassett, he used to train with Crokes and I liked him. I hate being marked by that guy so I'll take the lad I don't recognize. It was fucking Mike McCarthy.

'I remember it was the longest forty minutes of my life. I wasn't fit, I got absolutely fucking destroyed. He was coming over my shoulder, he was impossible to mark, and I think that was the death knell for me. I had one shot at goal, from the sideline, and hit the post. Gone. I did well to get that shot, I think he must have slipped. He was literally impossible to mark. I remember coming off the pitch totally deflated.' McCarthy went on to claim three All-Stars and four All-Irelands in a glittering career.

66

O'Keeffe believes that Carr failed him and some of the other fringe players. 'Carr never really talked to me, it was a weakness of that management panel. They didn't keep lads interested, always felt you'd know early on. Some lads are summer footballers, some winter, and in the position I was playing no one got a proper run. We were bitches when we couldn't get a game. We went up to Down [for a friendly]. Jim was playing and missing everything but he knew that, no matter how shit he played, he'd still get picked for championship.'

The Dubs easily overcame Longford in the Leinster quarter-final in Croke Park on 27 May, winning 2-19 to 1-13. In a one-sided contest, Johnny Magee did his bit to keep the Longford dangerman Paul Barden in check. The young star was going so well that Magee felt the need to begin roughing him up. Barden's brother David was having none of it, burying Magee with a shoulder. It sparked a verbal war between the players which escalated when Barden caught Magee with an elbow in the face. Magee waited for his moment, and that moment arrived when Paddy Christie collected a high ball and took off down the right-hand side of the pitch. The eyes of the officials elsewhere, Magee poleaxed Barden. 'There was blood pouring out of his face,' one of the other players recalls. 'Johnny says, "Don't be the big man up in Croke Park." We were sitting there in the players' lounge afterwards when Barden's girlfriend and mother came up and had a go. Johnny told them it was a big boy's game and you should finish what you start!'

Vinnie Murphy was back in blue, wanted by Carr for the havoc he could cause in a ten-minute spell late on in games. The often-maligned All-Ireland winner – he played in the final minute of the '95 final – had been ditched by Whelan but was back, following a spell playing club football in Kerry. He had toughened up during his time down the country, and became a fans' favourite. Murphy was the type of player who could be togging out for a junior football club match on a Sunday morning, and just before throw-in would approach his direct opponent for the customary handshake. He would offer his left hand, and his rival would reciprocate. Vinnie would then use his right hand to punch his man in the stomach. His job for Carr's Dublin, should the need arise, was to come on and throw his weight around. Dublin laboured to beat Offaly by 1-12 to 0-13 on 17 June in the semi-final, and it was the introduction of Murphy that got them over the line. He entered the Croke Park field, hopped off a few opponents, got the blood pumping and the fans singing, delivered two important points, and once more they were back in a Leinster final. Once more, the opponent was Meath.

With Davy Byrne injured, Carr gave a championship debut to Stephen Cluxton, a young keeper from Parnells, in the quarter-final, and played him again in the semi-final. Bizarrely, while Byrne was out, the sub keeper was none other than John O'Leary, aged forty, who hadn't played for Dublin since retiring in 1997. As O'Leary recalls, they kept his presence in the playing squad a secret at the time. He was togged out, but with a tracksuit on over his kit, and participating in the warm-up much as he normally would as goalkeeping coach, nobody seems to have noticed.

O'Leary was not named in the match-day programmes, but was listed as number 16 on the team sheets handed in to the referees for those games. He recalls, 'It was our secret, really. We discussed what we could do in the event of Stephen picking up a knock, and we decided I would be available if that happened. I would have kept fit by playing in the A v. B games in training, but only Dessie as captain knew. When Davy returned, Stephen went to the bench and nothing more was ever said. We never mentioned it for years afterwards.'

Carr, for his part, takes the view that even four years after retiring, the forty-year-old O'Leary was still 'the best keeper in Dublin'.

All week Carr's main concern had been over the fitness of Johnny Magee, after his centre half back was involved in a car accident. Dr Noel McCaffrey was called on to determine Magee's fitness to play and, with the player willing, gave him the nod. Magee struggled in the Royals' 2-11 to 0-14 win, which left the Dubs down — but this time not out. The GAA had finally brought in a back-door system so that the losers of provincial finals got another crack at the championship. The Dubs were going to get, as Keith Barr might say, a second bite of the fucking apple.

Dublin's first taste of the qualifiers was a confidence-building affair, overcoming Sligo by 3-17 to 0-12. O'Leary was back in retirement as a keeper, concentrating on his managerial duties. Carr felt his side were driven by a furious anger after the Meath game, at themselves and at the critics. And Dublin were also learning early back-door lessons. With the qualifiers not yet a week old, some teams were already complaining about the short turnaround times: the vanquished were sometimes given as few as six days to regroup and go again. Dublin's management team were determined not to sulk.

Their reward was an All-Ireland quarter-final against the defending All-Ireland champions, Kerry. It was the first time the ancient rivals had met in the championship since 1985, when the Kingdom claimed yet another All-Ireland title at the expense of the Dubs. The glorious August Bank

Holiday weekend in Thurles got off to a surreal start when the Dublin panel got word that the actor Colm Meaney was downstairs from their hotel. Vinnie Murphy, a big *Star Trek* fan, emerged from his shower and roared out the window: 'Beam me up, Scotty.'

Thousands of Dublin cars snaked down the N7, which felt to many fans like another galaxy. For many, time ran out and cars were abandoned; the pints would have to wait. It was business as usual early on, Dublin all endeavour with no end product as their stylish opponents barely broke sweat. Collie Moran had a horror miss when clean through, Farrell smashed one off the crossbar, and Whelan hit a post when going for goal. Kerry took their chances, sauntering in at half-time with a 1-5 to 0-3 lead.

And then, bedlam. Seven points down with just ten minutes to go, Dublin staged a heroic fightback in the Thurles sunshine. Goals from sub Murphy and Darren Homan, either side of a monster point from Whelan, gave the Dubs a one-point advantage going in to stoppage time. Then Byrne fluffed a goal kick-out over the sideline. It was still a good forty-five yards out, so plans were put in place to deal with the high ball in. Kerry wizard Maurice Fitzgerald had recently come on (and was immediately roughed up by several Dubs who would have preferred it if he was anywhere but there). He asked his manager Páidí Ó Sé what he should do, and Páidí casually asked him to just pop it over the bar. Elegant and deadly, he stepped up to take the kick. Carr did his best to put him off by delivering a few verbals in his direction, but Fitzgerald was in the zone. He bent it over with the outside of his right foot, equalizing with one of the great championship points.

Maurice's magic displayed Dublin's ineffectiveness from

placed balls in an even harsher light. Homan's fisted goal had come about from a forty-five-yard Wayne McCarthy free that dropped short. Following the Kerry equalizer, McCarthy had another one from similar distance to win it. It too had no legs, and the ball went behind for a 45. The young Erin's Isle man scuffed that one, too. Dublin's rally was the result of sheer resilience, not quality. They drove on as if their lives depended on it against superior opponents and, if it hadn't been for the dead-ball disasters, would have claimed an unlikely victory.

Homan occasionally watches those final minutes on You-Tube with his son, and while the lad loves seeing his dad fist home a goal to put Dublin into a late lead, the old man who could have been the match winner is full of regrets. He thinks of the bench, and the presence of a man who could have been called on to nail that late 45. He recalls: 'The funny thing about it, Stephen Cluxton was there. Even at that point he used to kick 45s in training. It was more for accuracy, but you say to yourself it would have been some brave call back then to bring him on. To take off a player and bring on a young Stephen Cluxton to take the last kick of the game.

'As it was, Wayne had the kick to win the game. I just said to him, "Put it over, son." I honestly thought he would. Wayne could be very good, at training he was very accurate. There was a bit of a breeze blowing into his face, though. You look back at these things. You watch the kick from Davy Byrne: if he'd kicked it down the middle it was 50/50 we'd have won it, but he just skewed it, it was a terrible kick-out. Little things like that.

'John O'Leary used to say to us, "You look at the match and someone kicks it wide in the first minute, no one has a problem with it. But you put the ball wide in the last minute when you're a point down, people remember it." But so much happened throughout that game that had a direct bearing. We missed so many chances.'

Carr says: 'We didn't have a free-taker, [McCarthy] wasn't Dean Rock. He was tier two. We didn't have the players, either – it's not making an excuse, but if we had a Diarmuid Connolly or a Paddy Andrews, go through the team sheet, any of them . . . Did we get the most out of the team? Absolutely. There wasn't another ounce left in them.'

For the replay, Carr was banished to the stands as punishment for his indiscretions in the drawn match (he had charged on to the pitch to confront the referee). From there he watched Johnny Crowley plunder two early goals. The champions outscored Dublin by 2-4 to 0-1 over ten pulsating first-half minutes to lead by 10 at the break. Tomás Ó Sé saw red early in the second half for a foul on Moran, and when Homan goaled on forty-six minutes the travelling Hill dared to dream. Late points from the dropped Wayne McCarthy, who came on as sub, brought Dublin close enough for late goal chances to matter. But neither Niall O'Donoghue nor Coman Goggins could capitalize, and it was all over for another year. Dublin, tank empty and hearts broken, were beaten by 2-12 to 1-12. The county chairman, John Bailey, went into the dressing room to declare his support for the manager.

Dessie Farrell was the only Dublin forward on the pitch that day who would have made it into the Kerry set-up. The manager had engendered a fighting spirit, fitness and camaraderie to match anyone's, but he could do nothing about the dearth of attacking talent.

In late September 2001, the county's Management Committee voted 4–3 against Carr retaining his position. This prompted the players to issue a statement slamming the 'shambolic' Committee and insisting: 'The players' support for Tom Carr and his selectors is total and unequivocal. The effort made by this sideline team on behalf of Dublin football has been monumental. Having taken charge during a transitionary and turbulent period they have now solid foundations in place on which to build and continue the development of the squad.'

The County Board delegates then held a second vote on 1 October; it finished 46 in favour of keeping Carr and 46 in favour of sacking him. Chairman John Bailey had the casting vote, and made his decision: Carr was gone. He learned of his sacking on the 9 o'clock RTÉ news.

Carr is adamant that Bailey told him all along his job was safe, even as late as the morning of the vote.

'I got a call from John that day and he said, "Look, there will be a vote but don't worry, it's sorted." I had said to the lads in Parnell, "Look, lads, I appreciate what you're doing, there's no need to go out on a limb on my behalf, I'm so fucking proud of you all. What you've shown me and what you're prepared to do is a payoff for me for the four years. Your loyalty and commitment to me can't be questioned, so whatever happens, fellas, I just want to thank you."'

He had made a goodbye speech in Thurles, just in case. He wondered if he had what it took to make a breakthrough after four gruelling seasons. 'Yes, we had taken Kerry to a draw, we had got to three Leinster finals, but we hadn't taken that final step. I kind of felt myself, "What will I do next year with a fifth year? Will it be any different?" So maybe I was even questioning myself. It was a little bit of a relief that the decision was taken out of my hands, if you know what I mean!

'It was a perfect stab in the back, a beautiful *Et tu, Brute*. I was sitting at home, it was on the main news, "Tommy Carr has been sacked" – and then the call came in afterwards. I said, "John, it said on the 9 o'clock news that you voted against me." And he started mumbling and I said, "You're two-faced, so dishonest, you're a liar."

'It was a short phone call. I hung up. I was fit to kill. And I haven't seen him since. I would have preferred if he'd sat down that morning to say, "Look, Tom, you've had four years and I can't really see the support." I'd say, "Look, John, that's fine, no problem as long as you're telling me now." But to tell me "I'll be supporting you" and then not to!'

Bailey, who is now a Fine Gael councillor in Dun Laoghaire-Rathdown, remembers that period differently. 'I told [Carr] way in advance that if things weren't going right I'd make changes,' he says. During the league campaign, Bailey says, he met with Carr at the Red Cow Hotel and told him he no longer had his backing. He says Carr asked for more time, and that he agreed. But once called upon to decide with his casting vote later that year, Bailey decided he had seen enough.

'It went to a vote and went to the casting vote and before I made the casting vote I asked the management [committee] if they wanted to change their mind, and they didn't.' In other words, they weren't letting Bailey off the hook; his vote would either save or doom Carr. 'You have to be able to stand up and make your decisions. There was no stabbing in the back. He got his time; it didn't work for him in the way he would have wanted.'

A furious O'Leary, Crean and Twomey came out in the weeks that followed and had their say on the decision that saw them lose their jobs too. They believed they were coaching a team that was on the up, unlike the bedraggled bunch they took over four years previously. They had pride in their achievements, and in the honesty of Carr's work.

The players were hurt, and almost to a man were deeply unhappy with Bailey's action in dismissing the boss. Collie Moran says: 'We were very loyal to Tommy. When you meet him today, even though it's not often, the players of that time would still have a lot of affection for him and admiration. He was a very tough guy, very strict, but had a good sense of humour, dry wit as well. Certainly at the end it was a disaster, the way he departed.

'The players weren't happy, they were disappointed. There was a very tight bond in the squad at that stage. While we did have good players, [if you] compare that to Meath and Kerry, there was a skills gap between the teams. Kerry had the real traditional ball-players, elegant, lots of scoring forwards, and we were a team at the time more about energy and passion, missing a couple of killer top-class forwards.'

Shane Ryan says: 'At the time I was devastated for Tommy. Every year I thought we were getting stronger and closer to winning Leinster. I would have felt good about him because he brought me into the squad, I felt a loyalty to him. What made it worse, having gotten so close to beating Kerry, we got emotional, thinking we were close to doing something huge. The Chairman at the time comes into the changing rooms after we were beaten and passionately declares his support for Tommy Carr, and we thought, "This is great, we're leaving here with a bit of positivity even though we're all gutted." And of course he stabs him in the back a few months later.'

Magee feels that he let Carr down by declaring himself fit to face Meath in the 2001 Leinster final. It was Meath, after all. A fortnight previously he had been in a car crash which put him and his daughter in hospital. He said: 'I shouldn't have played. I let Tommy down in that sense, should have been more honest. My head wasn't right. Another Leinster final against Meath, I wasn't at my fittest either, it was a bad day, should have put my hands up and said, "Sorry, I can't play," but pride got in the way, it overshadows your thought process.

'We should have beaten Kerry the first day. Second day we had our chances, Dessie and Collie hitting the post. We never seemed to have the luck, we had a strong team. John Bailey walked in, "I'm backing this man," tears in his eyes; then he left the room and we're all, "Where the fuck did that come from?" Then fast forward a few months and he's the one who casts the vote to get him out!'

Homan says: 'I loved playing for Tommy Carr. He was great. We just didn't get the luck to get over the line. Against Meath in that Leinster final, he'd been playing Cluxton, put in Davy Byrne and he made a mistake, Geraghty slid in, punches in along the ground and we were chasing that goal for the rest of the game. It all hinged on little things.'

O'Keeffe's take is a bit different. 'At that stage, the county board realized they needed to change something: Dublin were going nowhere. We'd got to a league final, won an O'Byrne cup; but in Dublin, after a very successful early '90s, to have no Leinsters even after five or six years was not good enough.

'The player revolt to keep him was self-preservation, if you ask me. A lot of the guys felt they weren't that far away, with the back door they were coming again, "Give Tommy another year," that kind of thing.

'It didn't work for whatever reason. We had the players. If they had taken a knife to the team, built it around Whelo, Robbo, Cossie and Christie, a completely new team, given it a year to fail rather than trying to patch up a team with half of them and half of us. It's hard to do – Dessie was still the best player, so not him, but other lads were coming to the end.

'He didn't have all the superstars, but lads didn't get the opportunity to be a superstar. Chopping and changing the team, nobody got a run of the fucking thing. Then you had the Wayne McCarthys and Vinnie Murphys and all that shite. If you look at it now, you're thinking what kind of fellas were they bringing into the Dublin team back then?'

Carr never marked his playing retirement with pints, and he politely declined requests for a night out after his sacking. The four years managing Dublin were the best days of his life. How does a man mark the end of that? Carr didn't set foot in Croke Park to watch Dublin for a decade afterwards. For a military man who organized a career around Dublin, not being there left a hole. He had never been able to take a break from his county commitments; now here he was, cast adrift at forty. On the outside looking in.

'Am I bitter now? No I'm not,' he insists. 'I'm regretful that we didn't make the breakthrough. That's my biggest regret, more than that I was fired. I got a multitude of phone calls from the players, but life moves on and I knew that at the time. They talked about organizing a night to say good-bye and I said I didn't want any of that stuff.'

Four years, and a lifetime of regrets that play over and over in his head. The early defeats Carr takes in his stride, but the other ones just won't go away. Sometimes he's taunting Maurice Fitzgerald in his dreams, but the Kerry conjuror never misses. 'We had been beaten by Kildare in the first, beaten badly by Meath, and then it looked like we were going to win at half-time in the third year. There were so many unlucky moments, Dessie missing a goal from three yards, Collie Moran hitting the fucking post from one yard, and that poxy Maurice Fitzgerald point.' Carr thinks Maurice Fitz stole a couple of yards. 'If you look at it again, the side-line was down here, he was fucking up there by the time he took the kick. These are the things nobody ever sees.

'Do I think about it? Absolutely! Davy Byrne kicking the ball over the line from a kick-out, all he had to do was kick out and play it around for a while and we'd have beaten Kerry in an All-Ireland quarter-final.'

Carr stopped going to the games. 'I found it too difficult, to be honest,' he says. 'I followed them, but after playing for ten years and managing for four and then to be going in at a turnstile and watching in a stand, nah, not for me. I'd say it was nearly ten years after that before I went back. I made myself busy because I had had Dublin football for fourteen years. It's a long time. Best part of your life. Sometimes I think I admire Jack McCaffrey being able to walk away from it; I wouldn't have been able to do that, I was addicted to it. I would like to have been able to walk away for two or three years, but my whole life was planned around Dublin football. Even in the army it was planned around Dublin football. My Lebanon trips were from October to March/April so I could come back and play championship football, all that stuff.

'My relationship with the supporters was super. They were always great to me; when it was going bad they were great to me. I love the Dublin supporters. They can be fickle, you saw it with Mickey and Lyons, but I didn't get that. They were very good to me and still are.

'Could we have regrouped and rejuvenated again? Absolutely. Am I going to be defensive about my time? Absolutely. Could I have been dealt a better hand? Yes. Could I have done things better or differently? Yes, I'm sure I could. I don't think I went outside of the current panel well enough to look for other players. I would have done that differently, spread the net wider. Now maybe they weren't there, but if they were there I didn't find enough of them.'

5. Minor Matters

Dublin's senior footballers were never really in control of their own destiny. Whichever manager took the team was a hostage to fortune, or grave misfortune. There was no conveyor belt of young talent.

Players like Jimmy Keaveney in the 1970s, Barney Rock in the 1980s and Dessie Farrell in the 1990s broke through to the senior ranks almost despite the system. Dublin GAA was built on a foundation of sand. It was not unusual to see even some of the bigger clubs operating without teams at several age groups.

Dublin's underage record was abysmal. In 1984, Dublin beat Tipperary by 1-9 to 0-4 in the minor football final. The county would not win another minor All-Ireland until 2012. At under-21 level, it was even worse: Dublin had never won an All-Ireland, and would not do so until 2003.

The mentality at underage mirrored that of the senior ranks: there were no second chances. Paddy Christie was one player who failed to impress in his shot at minor, and was almost lost to the game. Great GAA men kept him interested, but great GAA men can only do so much. Key club figures, such as Anto McCaul at Ballymun Kickhams, kept the flame flickering when a lack of cohesion at county level might have snuffed it out. Strip Dublin football of the passion of those few, and they might as well have dug a hole in the ground to dump the players patience forgot.

In the early 1990s, former county board chairman Jimmy

Grey and county official Donal Hickey led a small delegation to the offices of Bertie Ahern, who was Minister for Finance in Albert Reynolds' government. They asked him for money to redevelop the ramshackle Parnell Park in Donnycarney, then a gloomy and uninviting field surrounded by grassy hills, tin roofs and crumbling walls. The state of the place was symbolic of the state of Dublin GAA. It was also a real factor in holding back progress: a potential moneyspinner going to rack and ruin.

The redevelopment of Parnell Park was the first item in the in-tray of John Bailey, who was elected county chairman in 1994. The €3.3 million budget for the project was, in the end, funded from a number of sources. The Leinster Council provided a £500,000 loan, and Croke Park a £500,000 grant. Bertie provided around £400,000 from State coffers, and clubs paid contributions of anything from £2,500 (junior club) to £15,000 (senior club). Season tickets were sold in bulk to clubs, which then sold them on; the proceeds of this scheme were used to repay the loans.

Bertie – who as Taoiseach would later secure the grants needed to get floodlights installed – was present at the groundbreaking. 'They gave me a spade from the opening and I still have it,' he says. 'It's out in the shed with the other spades and every time I go to do work I think, "Jeez, I better not use that spade!"'

Bertie Ahern was steeped in Dublin GAA. A far better soccer player than footballer, he nevertheless spent his childhood weekends with his dad watching St Margaret's of the north county, and the students of St Pat's in his native Drumcondra. He stood as a boy on the Canal end, six steps down, because his dad was a country man. His brother Maurice rebelled, and watched from the Hill, where he continues to stand firm. The future Taoiseach witnessed the decline, and was there for the coming of Heffo. 'Kevin saved us from sinking,' he says. 'If it wasn't for him it would have been lost altogether, the game was dead. I mean, if ever there was a man who should be the uncrowned king of Ireland, it's Kevin Heffernan.'

In 1995, not everyone was buying the Jayo-inspired march to the final. Ahern recalls driving back to Dublin from Wexford on the morning of the All-Ireland final and not seeing a blue-and-navy flag until Binns Bridge in Drumcondra.

'People say now, "Aw, you have loads of population there" – well, we had loads then too, but we had no one playing GAA,' he says.

While Donnycarney was getting the necessary makeover, Bailey approached Bertie with another idea. He wanted to get more people playing Gaelic games and, just as importantly, he wanted it to be organized. Committed managers of underage sides had for too long been running all over the city, dragging their players out of bed. He found a sympathetic ear in the Finance Minister. Ahern was a product of the Christian Brothers in St Aidan's, Whitehall, where he was 'fucking leathered' by some of the teachers. His brothers had attended another GAA hotbed, O'Connell's, in the shadow of Croke Park. These schools, along with St Joseph's (Joey's) in Fairview and Ardscoil Rís in Marino, had been the backbone of GAA in Dublin. But times were changing, a rot was setting in. The finance minister and the county chairman met regularly for tea; Bertie would have preferred a pint, but Bailey was teetotal.

One of the things they talked about was the decline in the standard of coaching in schools. Bailey, Bertie and everyone else at the core of GAA in Dublin could see that teachers were putting in fewer unpaid hours after school. Standards were slipping.

'The difference between now and forty years ago, if you stood outside a school when the bell rang back then, you'd be run down by all the kids running home,' says Ahern. 'If you stood there now, you'd be run down by the teachers. So there are challenges, the world moves on. Who's going to train the team at half-four? The schools were collapsing, the clubs were collapsing. There was a handful of them doing well, but even some of the traditional ones were not doing well, St Vincent's for example. Thomas Davis had a good run for a while because there was a huge population in Tallaght and they won two or three championships, and Parnell's had a run although there wasn't too many Dubs. Erin's Isle had a great run because of all the Barrs that all came through together; but other than that all the north county ones, they were dying on their feet. Famous clubs like St Margaret's – who used to have the Monks, four or five of them on the team, they were big men . . . But all that was dead, and OK we did win in '95 and had that team, but other than that it wasn't a great scene. The thing was, the only way we could do this was to get the schools linked back to coaches, back linked with the clubs, revitalize the GAA in the city, try and get people behind the team.'

Ahern agreed to fund a coaching revolution in Dublin. Croke Park showed no interest at first. They were focused on the redevelopment of HQ. But eventually GAA bosses, worried about player participation level in the capital, warmed to the idea. The project was introduced on the basis that it was a pilot. If it worked in Dublin, it could be rolled out elsewhere.

'I could bring it through Finance because it involved coaching kids,' Bertie explains. 'It was school, it was afterschool . . . we had to gear the whole thing back to school because that was the only way I could justify it. I said it would have to be absolutely transparent and public, because I'd get hammered [otherwise], and that's what we did. We put it up as a pilot project, and I made a few speeches. I built it into the estimates that it was a pilot that would continue in Dublin, and if other people wanted to add in bits later on, fine, but Dublin would remain, and that's what I did. I did it on the basis that GAA in Dublin wasn't dead but it was weak.' By building the project into the estimates, Ahern ensured that the project was set in stone even if he moved out of Finance. Of course, the fact that he went on to be Taoiseach helped too.

Clubs were forced to adhere to strict rules in order to avail themselves of state aid. It took quite some time for the project to build momentum. Ahern explains: 'There was a lot of ad hoc-ery at the start, you had to convince the clubs. Bailey told them they could get a coach, but getting the money was very conditional, and [the conditions were] drafted up by civil servants, and rightly so. Clubs had to show how they were going to help with the primary school, the secondary school, and that they were going to talk to the community leaders in the place. It was all about building a network.' To Ahern it wasn't rocket science. He spent his holidays in Kerry, where they had been doing all that without State aid for generations. 'You have to butter the bread,' he says, 'before you put the sambo together.'

He and Bailey were on the same wavelength. 'Our biggest weakness was in coaching,' Bailey says. 'Where was the big advantage? Dublin was now becoming a fine city, with north

Dublin out to the Drogheda side rather than just north Fingal. We had south Dublin, Lucan, Tallaght, out to Shankill and Stepaside. I set about putting a plan together. It involved spending €2 million a year on coaches, who were paid €45,000 each.

That such a scheme was required was, in one way, an indictment of where the association was headed in Dublin. Volunteerism was in decline. The scheme could have been vulnerable to attack on the grounds that it was professionalizing work that had always been done on an amateur basis – and still was, in every other county. But external criticism was minimal – and Ahern knew how to keep resistance to a minimum. 'One of the reasons there was no criticism is because we were giving money to all the county grounds and all that worked very well,' he explains. 'Would they have been supportive if we weren't doing the county grounds and Croke Park at the same time? I don't know. Even the soccer and rugby lads didn't have too much to say.'

Ahern accepts that Dublin's revolution has left some people behind, none more so than the communities in Dublin's city centre. 'I was sad that it didn't work better within the canals,' Ahern says. 'Not just because it was my constituency. I would have prioritized there, and that still has to be done as it's still not good enough. There were huge areas within the canals that weren't developed and they were the areas that have the drug problems and the crime, and I still think more should be done in those areas. It's easy to go out to Malahide and Portmarnock, but it's not so easy to go into Sheriff Street and develop it. It can work but you need people dedicated.

'I watched a lot of kids grow up there and it's hard going. Some of the guys who go into crime, they're people who could be playing GAA, great tough players in those areas. Go back to the '40s and even at that stage we weren't getting the players from those areas. Paddy Cullen would have been an exception, but very few guys [were] coming from there and there hasn't been for two or three generations. Questions need to be asked, why is it an area so populated that we're not seeing come through. People will give you horse shit saying that these lads are being developed and then people come in and move them out to other clubs. No, I watched it for years, it's not happening.'

Amalgamations saw city-centre clubs move out to the suburbs: Eoghan Ruadh, where the Brothers once influenced, moved out to the Navan road to merge with St Oliver Plunkett's. The likes of Scoil Uí Chonaill in Clontarf, its roots deep in the north inner city where O'Connells stands, found it difficult for a long time to bring in the youngsters from those areas in anywhere near the same numbers.

'There are those who think the job is all done, and I don't accept it for a minute. When people moan about the crime and ongoing problems, I mean we put millions in there, more than goes in anywhere else, and Enda Kenny when Taoiseach said it last year when meeting residents about the Hutches and Kinahan thing.

'It's how it's spent, there's plenty of bloody resources going into it. If you don't interact, they suffer. Sometimes you have to pay coaches to come in. That's the way it is and that's after forty years of working on the ground there.'

'Dublin were brutal at minor level, under-21 they were a joke. Worse again,' says Mick O'Keeffe. 'It was literally who in Dublin wanted the job, put their hand up a couple of weeks out from the start of the championship. There'd be a trawl through minor squads, put a team together and hope they get through the first round.

'Back then the winning minor club manager would take the [county] team and they'd usually have seven or eight of that winning team on the team. That was the underage set-up.

'My minor manager in 1994 would have been Alan Larkin from Raheny. We had Robertson, Whelan, Sherlock and Cossie. We were the first decent minors in a while to come out of Dublin.' But there was a setback in 1997, when the Dublin under-21s got into a brawl against Offaly in Parnell Park. (In his autobiography, Jason Sherlock said he was spat on by a Dublin GAA official during the game. Players who were with him at the time had to be held back, by Sherlock himself, from tackling the official.) The county was hit with a two-year ban at under-21 level. 'That was a lost opportunity because that was a good team,' says O'Keeffe.

Christie was one of what would become a large group of past and present players – led by Stephen O'Shaughnessy and driven by John Costello – to get involved in moulding future generations. It was just about giving something back, only by doing it a little better. He didn't want anyone else who should be making it to miss out, like he almost did.

'My only recollection of some sort of county thing back then was a north Dublin trip to London with [Scoil Uí Chonaill coach] Gerry Rowley. One person was picked from each club, some of the lads who went weren't even that good, it was only a matter of who was sent. There was really nothing there. If someone was really good and they stuck out like a sore thumb at under-16, the following year they might be asked to come out for a trial even if they were too young.

'Having fifteen-a-side trials on a muddy pitch in January didn't lend itself to picking the best players. What inevitably happened was the strongest players from each team were usually midfielders; at the time that position was a huge deal, and a lot of clubs would just send those fellas so you found some of the county teams at minor level had two midfielders in the half back line and three in the half forward line. And then the two main lads themselves, and one thrown in at full back too for high ball.

'I was playing minor with Kickhams. We were a reasonably good team, a little thin on resources but we had some very good players, Ian Robertson for example. We played St Sylvester's in a minor Division 1 league game, a top-of-the-table clash. We drew, and we had no one on the panel. Sylvester's had ten. So, you know, they probably were a better team, but it was crazy that you could have that many from one team and none from the other that was reasonably equal, but that's just how it worked out.

'I went for a trial, I probably didn't play well in the one-off game, and that was it – you were gone then. There was no idea of development, no repeated shots, just one game. It was a disastrous system when you look at it.'

Having failed to make the Dublin minors, Christie went on to make the under-21s and, in short order, the senior team. He gives much credit for his quick rise to Anto McCaul, who coached the Kickhams' under-21s. 'If I didn't have Anto I probably wouldn't have played even senior with Kickhams – he just brought me on a tonne. He improved me as a player and kept me interested. He was passionate and pushed me very hard, and if you were going to miss a session for some silly reason he'd find a way to convince you not to.'

Development squads were up and running by 2001 and quickly evolved into a well-oiled machine. Every year they took in a hundred of the best footballers and a hundred

hurlers from twelve years of age to train as Dublin footballers, often under the tutelage of well-known Dublin stars. The
numbers in each age group got pruned back every year and,
where possible, each grouping remained under the guidance
of the same coaches all the way up. Though elitist by their
very nature, the development squads were also an attempt at
keeping players as close to their communities and roots as
possible. A centre of excellence, the likes of which would
eventually materialize in Kerry and Tyrone, was never part of
the thinking in Dublin GAA, and community-minded
Ahern for one reckons that's no bad thing.

Christie got involved in coaching almost from the moment
he broke into the senior team, overseeing summer camps to
earn an extra few bob, before moving on to the development
squads. He immediately recognized a cultural shift in the
organization of juvenile football in the capital. He said:
'Development squads are crucial in that they cut the unknown
out of the equation. You get good people involved, they pick
up fellas who are playing with a weaker or smaller club,
unlucky to have no good managers involved. That happens
regularly, but they now get sent to the development squads,
where they get that good coaching and get someone who is
motivated and is mad keen. Obviously what would be best in
the Dublin county scene is that every club would act as a
development squad – if that was to happen you'd be heading
towards complete world domination – but by the nature of
the club scene, it doesn't work that way.'

Christie was helped and influenced by his coach at under-
21 level, Dave Billings. 'When someone you respect comes
up and says if you put in more effort you can go all the way,
you start to believe. He gives you guidance. It starts to sink
in, then you play better, then you start seeing the jigsaw come

together. You need that little push. That's where the development squads come into play.

'It was the mid-'90s when I started doing coaching with the summer camps. The club started running summer camps and the county board started sending coaches around to individual clubs. The next thing was, they started having schools of excellence. U-13–U-15, a summer camp on a smaller scale with better coaches and more focused, less fun, deliberate practice.

'Then in the late '90s that evolved into the development squads as we know them. The county board recognized it was important to have people who had that experience, recognizable by young players, with some extra pedigree. It doesn't always work like that, there are some excellent coaches who've never played at a high level and there's no reason why that can't happen as well, but they made a conscious effort to get both past and current players to go around, and even if it was just signing t-shirts and saying a few words to each group and giving them a push, something like that was important, you know? They went down that path.'

Christie's club, Ballymun Kickhams, had long contributed important players to the county cause. Gerry McCaul played and then managed the Dubs to national league success in 1987. Barney Rock and Gerry Hargan in the '80s, Dermot Deasy and Ian Robertson in the '90s – all of them played a big part in Dublin's story. But organizationally it was haphazard, just like the majority of other clubs. Volunteers, with the best will in the world, could only achieve so much in the absence of better structures. When their emerging star defender took over an underage team, one he would manage for over a decade, he saw for himself the work that needed to be done. The learning curve was steep, the road travelled far from smooth.

A ten-year-old Philly McMahon would have no problem telling his manager to fuck off, or to disappear for weeks on end. The teacher, in the absence of a tutor, learned on the job.

'We were in a very bad way,' Christie says. I took over the U-10 team with Philly on it, and the 11s, 12s, 13s were non-existent. We were struggling to field teams, with no proper jerseys, and fellas were going out with Bermuda shorts. It was cringe.

'I took over U-10s because my brother was on it. I came up to see him train and ended up training him myself. That's how it often happens! Back then you couldn't get shorts. Nobody knew where to get them. Every so often someone would get their hands on a bunch but it was all over the shop. It's hard to believe now, but it was Stone Age stuff.

'We're not a superclub like Na Fianna or Ballyboden, we're medium sized. My son now, if he wants shorts or a club bag, I can ring a lady and she'll have it in two days. At that time, I didn't know where to get stuff. You had to go over to O'Neills, wait eight weeks to get it, but pay up front. I was twenty at the time. It was impossible. I had to go to county board meetings over in Oliver Plunkett's in Cabra, and sometimes I'd have to walk. It was archaic.

'My big thing was to try make them look the part, then make sure they were well coached. When they got to U-12 it dawned on me they were quite good. What was coming behind wasn't great, what was ahead was weak. What needed to be done in a semi-pro way was to find good people to take over those things to try spruce things up. I'd come out myself and try take some sessions with other teams. I'm not sure looking back if that was the right thing or not but I said I'm going to take this team and make sure as many as possible come through.'

New players like Mayo minor James Burke were attracted to Kickhams by a set-up that only a few years previously wasn't much to look at. Christie says: 'Fellas like James Burke joined a lot easier if the training and the set-up was good, and we showed a bit of pride. When fellas had a tracksuit and a gear bag they looked the part. That's what I tried to change. We looked better. Until then we were Ragball Rovers.'

Bertie's proximity to the Dubs ensured that some of the world's sporting and political elite were kept up to date with their affairs. He brought Alex Ferguson and his entire Manchester United squad to Croke Park in the summer of 1994 to see Dublin claim the Leinster championship. It was all kept under wraps, so that the Red Devils could enjoy a day out of the spotlight, following the previous day's friendly match against Dundalk. First stop was Dublin Castle, when an excited Fergie spent twenty minutes explaining the importance of James Connolly to his bored squad. The likes of Gary Pallister, Steve Bruce, Eric Cantona and Peter Schmeichel were somewhat more impressed with the GAA action. 'Pallister and Brucey couldn't believe that these guys were amateurs,' Bertie says. The team paid a secret visit to Temple Street after the game. Schmeichel was particularly taken with one sick child, and went out to get his gloves from the team's coach. He was spotted, and by the time the players left the hospital the 'entire north inner city was there to see them'.

By the time Ahern was forced to step down as Taoiseach in 2008, the job of modernizing the structures of Dublin GAA was pretty much done. The Dubs were done with leaving anything to chance. Sam would come home again, only this time not by accident.

6. Bringing Back the Buzz

Tommy Lyons took over as Dublin manager for the 2002 season. He had come very close to landing the job years before. Following the departure of Pat O'Neill in 1995, Lyons had been told the job was his – days before Mickey Whelan came from nowhere to land it. Lyons had shown his quality that year by leading Kilmacud Crokes to All-Ireland club glory and had fans on the county board. But he missed out, and was annoyed for a while – then moved on to Offaly, where he performed miracles. He was passed over for Tommy Carr, too.

And then, six years after someone in the chain of command at Dublin HQ broke their word, Lyons was given the job for the 2002 season. Ironically enough, he got the job only after O'Neill – who had been keen to return to the hot seat – withdrew for work reasons. Lyons impressed the decision-makers in the job interview, insisting he would tear up the playbook and start again. It was, he said, the only way for the team to succeed. The manner of Carr's sacking alarmed him greatly, and he took the job with a strict caveat: it wouldn't end that way for him. 'Ye won't stab me in the back.'

Two realities marked the new Dublin manager out from previous incumbents. One was his place of birth, the other his unremarkable footballing pedigree. Lyons hails from Louisburgh, an 18th-century planned town near the southern shore of Clew Bay, more than a few throws of a stone from Parnell Park. He moved to the capital at the age of ten, when his dad migrated for work reasons; but some people always viewed him as a Mayo man, most noticeably so when things weren't going well. And not only was he not from Dublin; he wasn't a Dub. Injuries wrecked his playing career before it really began. He was a culchie who played for and managed the culchies in Kilmacud. But he did well there. He did well in Offaly. We're in the fucking doldrums. Let's see what this guy can do for us.

Lyons took over in November 2001 on a three-year term, backed up by Paul 'Pillar' Caffrey, Dave Billings and Paddy Canning. The playing squad was running out of All-Ireland winners, but that was fine by him. He told the county board he didn't want to hear a peep of dissent from them for six months. He had a new squad of players to bed in, and it was going to take a while. Some league games would have to be sacrificed in the pursuit of progress.

Lyons's eyes were on the future, and that meant Alan Brogan. It meant Stephen Cluxton, Barry Cahill, Darren Magee and Paul Casey. Lyons wanted natural footballers, lashings of pace, and confident men who could thrive in the goldfish bowl. The management team set up trial games – first against Westmeath, where they laid an admiring eye on Cahill, and young David Henry from Raheny. Lyons also had big plans for one of Tommy Carr's cast-offs, a guy he'd known since he was a child, a guy who hadn't played for his county since being hauled off in the 1999 Leinster final shortly after he was brought on as a substitute. He reckoned his first season managing the Dubs, with quick ball-in and pacy forwards, was made for Ray Cosgrove.

Lyons had been watching the Dubs from afar and had seen the famous swagger morph into a depressing stagger. He decided he'd do whatever he could to bring the buzz back himself. Talk it up, sell the product, get the eyes fixed intently on you. It was time to embrace the hype.

'I was very disappointed about how Tom Carr's time ended,' he says now. He was walking into a dressing room of players who had gone out on a limb for the last guy, and many of them didn't want the new guy.

'I took a calculated gamble that I had to rebuild confidence,' he explains. 'Dublin hadn't won Leinster since '95, and seven years was an incredibly long time for a county like Dublin, like Kerry going seven years in Munster, and the confidence levels had gone way down. Even players coming in were affected by it.'

He called on his many contacts in business to contribute towards the Dublin cause. Several high-profile businessmen – dubbed 'the Taliban' by the players – donated substantial sums which helped Lyons put together the type of programme he couldn't have dreamed of with Offaly.

Lyons had a way with words. Writing in the match programme for the 2002 league opener at Parnell Park, he said: 'I am well aware that a pat on the back is only a foot away from a kick in the arse, probably closer when you are someone my size, but I would ask everyone to be patient over the coming months as many young players are given jerseys for the very first time.'

Even while continuing to pen a column for the *Evening Herald*, Lyons ordered his own players not to read anything about themselves in the media. Some of them took his orders to heart; Paddy Christie for one never read another word written about himself for the rest of his career.

In that league opener against Donegal, Lyons unveiled what would become for a time a fearsome full forward line: the returning Cosgrove, the tireless Johnny McNally and the gifted young Alan Brogan. Ciaran Whelan moved to the 40 to accommodate Darren Magee, whose brother Johnny was relegated to the bench. McNally's clubmate from Ballinteer St Johns, Coman Goggins, joined Henry in the full back line, and Cluxton took his place between the sticks. With Jim Gavin on the bench and Sherlock and Farrell not in the matchday squad, only Paul Curran remained from the class of '95. Brogan registered 1-3 in a 2-10 to 0-14 win, Cosgrove chalking up 3 points. Johnny Magee came off the bench to score Dublin's other goal.

Brogan and Cosgrove hit 1-3 apiece the following week as Dublin ran Tyrone close in Dungannon. It was a Tyrone of Canavan, O'Neill, McMenamim, McAnallen, Jordan, McGuigan and Cavanagh. Their paths would cross again. A draw in Tullamore with Offaly in which Brogan, McNally and Cosgrove hit 0-9 of Dublin's 10-point total meant it was a decent start to life for the new manager. And it was already clear which players were making the difference.

'I always was amazed at how Cossie had never made it,' says Lyons now. 'I saw him as a young fella in Crokes and he was an incredibly skilful player. It clicked for him that year. He struggled after that again, but Cossie was really as good a footballer as Dublin ever produced. Skilful, he had left and right feet, pace, could win a ball over his head. He was over six foot tall, had all the requirements to make it at the top level and to me I very quickly zoned in that Croke Park was a place where you needed pace and if you didn't have pace you'd be found out.

'Johnny McNally was a fantastic man, he emptied his tank for you every time. Bull strong, he reminds me of Eoghan O'Gara today, and you need these kinds of players. When you have a Cosgrove and a Brogan, you do need to have other types of player around. Johnny was as much a reason Ray had a great year as Ray was, as he took on a lot of heavy lifting.'

Lyons took to the younger players immediately and set about making them the core of his team along with Christie and Ciaran Whelan. It meant he persevered when mistakes were made – a change from the days when one mistake was all it took to kiss goodbye to a run in the Dublin team. The same patience didn't extend to some of the older warhorses, but the fall-out from that didn't begin to manifest until the following season. In 2002 – even as the league form began to disintegrate – everything seemed rosy.

Cosgrove was loving life in blue again, having been invited back by Lyons.

'A few years had passed, I was playing good football with the club, and Tommy would have known me inside out so I was only too delighted at that stage. When he threw me the jersey that first day in the national league he said, "You're getting that jersey, you don't have to look over your shoulder. You're going to be an integral part of my plans, you don't have to be worrying when you have a nightmare, I'm not going to drop you, you won't go back to the bottom of the pecking order." He believed in me. That's a massive show of confidence. He'd ring me the Monday after a game saying, "Cossie, you did this well, you did that poorly" or whatever, we had a good, honest, open relationship. If parts of my game were poor on a Sunday we'd have that chat, he'd tell me if I didn't see the right ball or if I shot off balance or whatever.

'My confidence grew. I had that luxury, having known him personally, that he could tell me what was what. Aspects I could improve on. That's the difference: I understood where he was coming from and paid him back in spades throughout the year. Alan had his first year, Johnny Mac was getting a run at it, we knew we were getting an opportunity, we had no hang-ups. Alan was young and cutting loose, I felt I had a little bit to prove, Tommy understood what I was about.'

Christie had been around since 1996, quietly going about his business. He never said it at the time, but he felt enormous pressure at full back during the 1990s. He felt that one mistake and Dublin were finished, because they lacked the top-class forwards necessary. He said: 'I look at the teams I was on, and I look at this modern-day team with great envy, because we had huge problems up front. Dessie was sometimes on his own, and those were the days before blanket defences. We just didn't have anyone. Once he was man-marked, we were in trouble. If we were playing now, we'd be walloped because teams would put three back on him and completely wipe him out. Sometimes Ian Robertson would play full forward and he was a good player, he was a target man, but if he was taken out of the equation we just didn't have the same strength.

'Charlie Redmond finishing up also hurt us badly. Because even though he was contributing very little from play near the end, his free-taking was phenomenal. For years we struggled to have a really reliable one. That was another issue, but we just didn't have dangerous forwards. When Ray and Alan exploded in 2002 it changed the whole thing around because for the first time in your life you felt a little more at ease playing there, thinking, "OK, if someone scores a goal against us we might not be able to get one in the other end."'

During a training session early that summer in St David's in Artane, Brogan, playing corner forward for the A team, found himself on the ball forty metres from goal. He flipped his man, used his distinctive hop to take out another couple, and before anyone on the B team knew what was happening the ball was in the net. Players looked at each other and nodded.

'I remember saying to myself, "He's going to cause some problems,"' says Christie. 'No end of hassle. Nobody really knew about him, I thought, "He's going to give somebody an awful going over." He turned the place upside down, he gave Meath an awful run around. He picked up balls for fun and was a good finisher. He had been playing in defence for a few years at underage. Tommy put him in where he belonged.'

The players recognized the need to keep an eye out for their prized asset. Brogan was young, emerging and enjoying life in the goldfish bowl. After matches in the summer of 2002, the Dubs ate dinner in Jury's Hotel before the trip to Coppers. Magee was the man in charge of the free drink tokens: a fairly generous ten per player. His orders were simple: of all the envelopes in his possession, the ones he had to ration most carefully were Brogan's.

Dessie Farrell, still regarded by most within the camp as the finest player in the squad, wasn't yet old. But he was injury-prone, and he wasn't the kind of player that Lyons necessarily needed. Lyons says: 'Certainly I never saw the best of Dessie. He was an incredibly committed player to the Dublin cause, but he had a body like a forty-year-old trying to play football. That was just the facts of it. Maybe I was one of the few people to say it straight to Dessie, and if I had him as a twenty-three-year-old he'd be on any team I'd ever pick.'

Farrell was a driving force behind the fledgling Gaelic Players Association. In 1999 a group of players, including Tyrone's Peter Canavan and Fergal Logan, got together to campaign for improved conditions for county players. Farrell was the first chairman the following year, and by 2003 he would be full-time chief executive. The GPA set up sponsorship deals for star names in direct contravention of GAA rules. The GAA introduced player entitlements the following year on foot of union pressure, providing for the first time structured mileage rates, better equipment, sustenance and conditions for players. It wasn't always plain sailing.

Lyons recalls: 'I got a call from a very senior county board official about Dessie when he got into the GPA to say I had to get rid of him off the panel. And equally I said very straight to him that Dessie will go off the panel when I think he's not good enough.'

Johnny Magee was another whose relationship with Lyons spanned many years. Magee once turned out for the Offaly B team against the A contingent when Lyons was boss, during the summer of '97. Lyons, who threw his young clubmate a few bob for his troubles, joked that Offaly wanted him permanently. ('No bleedin' way' was the predictable response.)

But things did not get off to a great start between the two when Lyons took over. In the intervening years, whatever credit Magee had in the bank from that history seems to have been spent. Magee had yet to hear from the new Dublin boss in any capacity when a journalist contacted him. 'That was my first interaction with Tommy as manager: a reporter telling me I'm out of the squad if I don't lose weight,' he says. 'He asked, "Do I care to comment?" I said, "No I don't, it's fucking bollox."'

Magee had missed three months of the previous season. Recovery was slow enough, and he reckoned he was carrying half a stone. As Magee remembers it, Lyons plonked his centre half back on a scales, and judged the excess baggage to be more like two stone. The Crokes man recalls that he was weighed religiously when most of the other players were not. In time, weighing players before and after training would become as routine as stretching hamstrings. In those days, it didn't happen – and certainly not focused on just one member of a squad. At one point, Lyons sent Magee to a businesswoman called Celia Larkin – better known as the partner of the then Taoiseach, Bertie Ahern. Larkin offered the footballer some nutritional advice. With him for company was Pillar Caffrey, who was overseeing the unorthodox visits on behalf of the manager, losing a few pounds himself in the process.

Magee dropped half a stone, prior to a league match against Offaly, started the game and earned some plaudits. After the game Lyons gave his players permission to go for a few drinks, with a strict caveat to take it very easy as they had training the following day. Magee had a few pints at a family event. Lyons got wind that some of his players were on the tear, and at training in Cathal Brugha barracks he asked them out straight.

Magee told his manager he'd had four pints. Lyons exploded. 'Four pints? A few is two or three,' he told him. 'Get your fucking gear bag and get the fuck out.' Magee was told not to come back until the following Tuesday. They spoke on the phone the following evening, Magee insisting he was being made a scapegoat when a much larger crew had been on the tear elsewhere.

Certainly there was a lack of mutual trust. Lyons reckoned the defender was feasting on fish and chips and any other take-away grub that took his fancy; Magee furiously disputed this. Lyons claims he never intended to make Magee feel singled out, and says: 'I liked Johnny Magee a lot as a footballer. I liked his heart and his desire and his way of going about it.

But Johnny and I disagreed over how you get ready for a big game. That's it in a nutshell.'

Lyons's first season in charge was shadowed by an off-field controversy: Croke Park was looking at splitting Dublin in two.

Starting in 2001, the Strategic Review Committee under Peter Quinn was tasked with creating a blueprint for the GAA in the 21st century. One branch of the SRC recommended dividing Dublin's senior football team into north and south by 2005. The stated aim was to increase participation in the capital. But the proposals lacked any sort of cohesion or common sense – and participation was on the up anyway. The suspicion was that the real reason for the proposal was a fear that Dublin would soon be too strong. Supporters were apoplectic, and the clubs were unanimous in their rejection of the GAA's proposals.

Bailey says he was a key man in rejecting a change that would not only have seen the county board structure altered, but his own power diluted. 'I could never divide Dublin,' he says. 'Dublin has its own uniqueness, its own character. North and south, there's a rivalry, an intensity, a passion and a loyalty that galvanizes Dublin as one county. They wanted to put Nicky Brennan in as co-chairman of Dublin; I said no. Or Seán Kelly; I said no.

'In a meeting at Croke Park which the government had a representative at I got up and walked out. I said, "No, you're not dividing Dublin. Over my dead body you're not, full stop." And they didn't do it. The county would have been split in half if I hadn't said no.'

In the summer of 2002, Dublin was buzzing again like it was 1995, 40-foot Boys in Blue posters taking pride of place on

O'Connell Street in the same year that construction finally began on the Spire.

Memorable campaigns can begin in the most inauspicious places, so Dr Cullen Park in Carlow was as good a place as anywhere to start the 2002 summer season. It wasn't Meath, or Kildare, or even Laois that Dublin faced in the Leinster quarter-finals on 1 June, but Wexford, who had limped out of the senior football championship the previous season in the first round of qualifiers.

(Dublin fans had form when it came to taking on Wexford away from Croke Park. At Wexford Park, during the 1993 championship, some supporters had taken over scoreboard duties – and one of them fell through the dressing-room roof. Legend has it that as he dragged himself up off the floor, he assumed a fighting stance and invited the Wexford masseuse to come have a go. Billy Walsh, an Olympic boxer in giving a dig-out to his native county, wisely warned him against it and the Dub was invited to leave. 'Up the Dubs,' he roared as he walked out.)

The match between Lyons's young guns and their Division 2B opponents crept up with little fanfare, and wasn't even the most important sporting event of the day to many of the crowd that made the short trip to the east midlands.

Ireland's international soccer team was in Japan for the World Cup, that morning opening their campaign with a 1–1 draw against Cameroon. The game kicked off at 7.30 a.m. Irish time, and for many fans that posed a quandary: push through from the night before, or get up and start drinking early? The travelling Hill 16 support put in a spirited display, and five of them took advantage of the warm weather to parade naked around the pitch. That was as good as the spectacle got, the lads on the field never quite getting to the pitch of the support roaring them on.

Brogan, Casey and Cahill made their championship debuts in a team skippered by Coman Goggins. At the end of seventy minutes, the Dublin manager was saying a silent prayer of thanks for Casey, who changed the course of the summer with a remarkable late block to deny Mattie Forde what would have been a winning goal. 'Sometimes you're in the right place at the right time,' he says modestly now.

The players weren't convinced they were making progress. Shane Ryan was buzzing at the prospect of playing centre forward for the first time in his Dublin career, and he felt the changeover in personnel was welcome. But something wasn't right. Collie Moran was one of just two starting forwards who had survived from the team that played against Kerry the summer before – the other being Dessie Farrell – and the feeling among some of the older hands was that too much was being changed too soon.

Occasionally, when poring over the carcass of the past, the main characters disagree on which parts to dissect. The team's training sessions at Leopardstown racecourse, in the days after the Wexford match, became infamous; those who weren't present struggled with visions of thoroughbreds Whelan, Christie and Cluxton clearing hurdles around one of the country's premier racetracks. Moran remembers it as hell on earth.

'We trained in Parnell in summer and Cathal Brugha in the winter. Then, on the June Bank Holiday, bodies tired after a close game, Tommy had us up at 6 p.m. the next evening in Leopardstown. He ran the hell out of us to the point of collapsing; then we finished up and he said, 'OK good session, back here tomorrow at 6 p.m.' So we spent the Bank Holiday dreading what's coming again. He had never done that before.'

Those within Lyons's coaching set-up remember it differently. One says: 'The point of Leopardstown was to help bring the players down to earth, to get them away from the hysteria. There were three sessions there in total, spread over the summer, all ending with a spell in the sauna and a meal. It was a bit of craic.'

A sense of foreboding and a date with old rivals Meath don't make for good bedfellows, but that was Dublin's reality as they faced into the provincial semi-final with the defending Leinster champions in Croke Park on 23 June. It was a red-letter day in GAA history, the almost completely redeveloped Croker reopening for the battle of two old foes. Nostalgic fans with a passion for the heavenly days of the recent past stopped moaning about Wexford and began dreaming again. They thought of Barr, Mick Lyons, Charlie Redmond, Brian Stafford, Barney Rock and David Beggy. They remembered the warriors who had made this fixture great and turned Gaelic football on its head. An appreciation of that shared history and an anticipation of what could be saw 63,000 paying customers swarm into HQ, given a striking new symmetry by the rebuilt Hogan Stand.

Those present witnessed a reawakening that signalled there could be good times ahead. Lyons's men out-fought, out-muscled and out-thought their more illustrious rivals, putting down a marker on the new playing surface in the opening seconds, when one of the players flattened Meath's John Cullinane, who was stretchered off with concussion. Geraghty and Giles, tormentors-in-chief in seasons gone by, were roughed up at different stages of the game as Dublin laid down their new law.

There was a refusal to bend, even to science. With just minutes on the clock, Johnny Magee hurt his knee in a challenge with Donal Curtis. Dublin's physio James Allen's on-pitch analysis told him he thought Magee's cruciate might be gone. Magee got up and soldiered on anyway. At half-time he was told to forget about playing on, but he went back out anyway, dosed up on painkillers. He wasn't going to miss this one. 'I had played at that stage in eight Leinster finals in various ages and Meath had beaten us every time. There was one point in the second half I kicked the ball and I swear to god I thought I was gonna find my fucking leg in the Cusack stand. I could hear Heery: "Get up, get up, it's Meath, get up." Heery was pulling me by the scruff. "Don't let anyone see you hurt." I was thinking, "He's up in the stand, I'll see him later in Fagan's pub or somewhere and he'd grab a hold of me!" It was that drive and determination, the will to win, no way they were going to beat us again.' Later on he'd learn that he'd torn his lateral collateral ligament, and damaged the cruciate; it was only the muscles in his legs that were holding his knee together.

The topsy-turvy nature of senior championship football at that time was manifested in the fact that none of the previous year's provincial winners would retain their titles. The old order was in flux, and it would take a few years to figure out who the new kingpins would be. Geraghty credited Lyons for the turnaround. 'Tommy, he knew what it took to win All-Irelands at club level and Leinster with Offaly, he had that swagger about him which you need in a manager. He was confident, arrogant in a nice way – he always thought he was going to win and he instilled that in the players. It definitely was a kick-start for them, and our downfall in a way.'

Moran was euphoric. OK, so Dublin hadn't won anything yet, but as a player you learn to cherish the good days. He says: 'We were coming in under the radar against Meath, they were still a top team, got to the final the year before and won in '99. Alan had a good day, Ray had a good day, I had a good day and kicked a fair few scores. That game is still a highlight for me when I look back. That's how you were measured as a Dublin footballer back then, how you did against Meath. If you kicked 5 points against Westmeath or Louth in a semi they'd still be waiting to see how you did against Meath to come to a conclusion about whether they rated you as a footballer or not.'

After a display like that, a team is often at its most vulnerable; but the Dubs backed it up with a 2-13 to 2-11 Leinster final win over O'Dwyer's Kildare in front of 78,033: payback for seven years of hurt. Second-half goals by Brogan and Cosgrove kept Dublin alive when their backs were to the wall, and Cluxton was then called upon in injury time to prevent what would have been a Kildare equalizer. To a man the players answered the call – Brogan immaculate, Christie imperious, and Whelan inspirational late on. Goggins became the first Dub since John O'Leary to lift the Delaney cup over his head.

The backdrop was different from before, the shiny new Hogan a symbol of the game's, and the team's, glittering future.

The deposed Carr, on a self-imposed exile from Croke Park and all things Dublin, couldn't help but feel numb, almost empty. 'It was a killer, genuinely it was a killer, so I don't mind saying it,' he reveals. 'I was delighted for the personnel, the fellas on the team, and I was delighted for the likes of Cluxton. They deserved it, and so did I. But it didn't happen.'

*

On 5 August, when Dublin played Donegal in the All-Ireland quarter-final, Tommy Lyons was missing from the Dublin bench. The manager had fallen ill while playing golf the previous day. Rumours spread like wildfire, to the extent that the Taoiseach is said to have told Fine Gael leader Enda Kenny, on his arrival at Croker, that Lyons had suffered a heart attack. His absence was put down at the time publicly to an unspecified illness, but the players believed that Lyons was in serious trouble. Lyons, who watched the game hooked up to machines from his bed in the Blackrock Clinic, was in fact suffering from gallstones. Caffrey was left to steer the ship in his absence.

Dublin struggled at times in the first half, a Cosgrove goal giving them the slenderest of half-time leads. Cluxton again showed what he was about with a brilliant second-half save, before the arrival of Jayo and Dessie from the bench added some vigour to an attack that was beginning to wilt. With six minutes left on the clock, Cossie again fired home, following great work from Sherlock. But Donegal hit three unanswered points to force a replay.

In the replay, with Lyons back in the saddle, Dublin demolished their northern opponents in a furious display marked by another exquisite goal from Cosgrove. The Hill was hopping and Dublin were untouchable. It really didn't get much better than this. Armagh would later eventually overcome Sligo after a replay. So: beat Armagh, and we were back in the final. That was the thought preoccupying the minds of supporters – the full-time ones, and those card carrying members of the bandwagon club who helped swell the quarter-final crowds to 77,000.

Cossie was getting noticed everywhere he went. He'd been a long time waiting for overnight success. His goals, and his celebrations, were being beamed into most homes in the country. Everyone knew him, and everyone wanted a piece of him, but it took him a long time to realize how big he'd become. He says: 'After we won the Leinster title you could sense a buzz about the place. The flags and bunting were up, a bit of razzmatazz had returned about the place. Bank of Ireland were doing their big poster on O'Connell Street, you could sense around then it was different to previous years. We hadn't seen it in so long.

'My stupid goal celebrations became a thing – there was a World Cup that year. I come from a soccer background, I played it most of my life. When I joined Crokes at U-15, I was predominantly a soccer player who'd just given the school team a dig-out, and it snowballed after that. The celebrations were a release of childhood dreams. I was on Hill 16 in '95, I was a fan until you start playing and the shoe is on the other foot. All that was going on, I'm a humble fella, I wasn't going out of my way looking for attention. I don't crave attention and looking back I was probably blind to it to be honest, it's not till you reflect and say, "Jaysus I had an unbelievable year." You're engrossed in it, cocooned in it. My life revolved around training five or six days a week, you weren't out getting all the plaudits, out with lads buying pints all the time.

'The few times you were out you had a good cut at it, you were kinda oblivious to the attention, and only when you step back and see the lads winning All-Irelands now do you think, "God, was I getting that sort of attention back then? Was I that popular?" I was oblivious, it didn't consume me. I was a little naïve to realize how big a name I'd become in the game, you're being invited to this, that and the other. I got a lot of media gigs, golf days, out to Áras an Uachtaráin, winning All-Stars, top scoring in championship. When you say it now you say I must have been stupid not to see it, but when you're not out Friday night in that environment getting claps on the back you don't necessarily see it. My Friday nights were at home resting up.'

Dublin were favourites against Armagh on 1 September. The Orchard County had struggled past Sligo and the hype machine was cranked up, with the mouth-watering prospect of a Dublin–Kerry final in three weeks' time. Armagh led for just eight of the seventy-four sun-drenched minutes played, six of those towards the end. Ciaran Whelan's devastating goaled response to Paddy McKeever's 3-pointer in the second half was a microcosm of a game in which neither side was able to pull away. Cosgrove was Man of the Match, firing over 4 points from play and a further 2 from frees in a masterclass of forward play. But his place in infamy was assured when his last-minute free, thirty yards from the Hill 16 goal, struck a post.

Armagh, deservedly, were into a final. There they would beat Kerry to claim their very first All-Ireland title, and bring the Ulster revolution to the masses. Dublin, once they managed to drag themselves off the turf and into the sanctuary of the dressing room, had much to be proud of. For now, though, they were once again battling that familiar feeling which came with being part of a Dublin team that hasn't quite made the grade.

Armagh's defender Justin McNulty recalls, 'We didn't care about the Dublin hype. We were very much focused on ourselves, knew that Dublin had easily overcome us in the encounters up to that point. In the league games we were competitive enough but Dublin were able to coast over us in the end. I'll never forget Whelan's goal in the semi-final. He was the marquee midfielder of that time, along with Darragh

Ó Sé. He was a colossus, a lot of people thought he was unmarkable. Unstoppable. Ray was on fire too, we knew that, so we knew we had a job on our hands to minimize their scoring threat. Again we got the luck of the green when Ray hit the post in the last minute. If it went to a replay, you have to say favourites more often win replays and it's unlikely we'd have won the replay, so the miss was crucial.'

In the near future, as sledging crept into the game, players in Cosgrove's position might expect to hear the virtues of his mother or another female relative being questioned. But not this time. He had nobody in his ear. McNulty says: 'That wouldn't have been our style. Our team weren't like that, we were hard and tough but there were no players who were annoyers, people like [Tyrone defender] Ricey McMenamin, we didn't have that kind of player. We may have done a few high tackles, late tackles, dirty tackles, or retaliate or get sent off, but there were no mouthpieces and there weren't too many other players we played against either who'd be like that.'

Cossie still thinks about that kick from time to time. 'I'd won the free,' he says. 'Darren Magee was the closest player to me. I'd kicked 6 points, it wasn't Geezer [Kieran McGeeney] or Francie [Bellew] in my ear, or the McNulty boys; I was simply too cautious. I won Man of the Match that day, but I will always be remembered for hitting the post. I didn't think twice, I didn't look around to throw the ball to Dessie or Declan Darcy, I wanted it. I was flying it, it was one of the best games I ever played in a blue jersey. If that kick was five minutes into the game I'd have drove it forty yards into Hill 16. Whether it went through the posts is a different story. I'd made up my mind as it was coming to injury time that I'd curl it inside the right post as I was looking at it because you couldn't be really aggressive. If you didn't make proper contact you'd look an absolute fool, so I said I'd use the instep to curl it around and unfortunately it didn't come in enough.'

Darren Homan blames himself for failing to anticipate the rebound off the post. 'We all thought it was going over. Why were none of us inside so we could have fisted it over the bar?'

After a barbecue summer, the Dubs' dreams were back in cold storage. No Dublin squad had ever been as prominent in the public eye, and it took a while for some to come back down to earth. Others, such as Paddy Christie, moved on immediately.

'I remember in 2002, the Leinster final was being shown on TV in October or November and I walked into the sitting room and my dad said, "You're just in time, they're showing this." I looked at it for about ten seconds and just turned and walked out. For me, when the game is played it's over. I didn't want to be living in the past. I know some people, they told me themselves they still watched games on video years later and I didn't want to be that person. For me it was a lovely memory but I didn't want to be looking back, I wanted to be looking forward. In 2002 I won All-Star, Leinster championship and played for Ireland in International Rules and I wanted to do that again the following year. Except now I'd be aiming for an All-Ireland. Build on what I'd done. So the best thing to do was forget about 2002. 2003 was a new year.'

7. Human Pyramids

The end to Tommy Lyons's reign has often been character-
ized as a great implosion, a revolution occasioned by the very
elements that shook the Dubs from their slumber in the first
place. It has been said that his team ignored (or was power-
less to heed) the warning signs, sleepwalking into oblivion,
taken down by a catastrophic mix of complacency and hubris.
The endgame unfolded over two years and produced some
of the darkest episodes in the county's history.

In January 2003, the Dubs found themselves in the same
hotel on their post-season holiday in South Africa as the
Kerry footballers and Kilkenny's hurlers. They tended to
avoid Brian Cody's Cats, but let their hair down with their
Kerry counterparts whenever their paths crossed. A sun-
burned Páidi Ó Sé had both tribes in stitches when he swam
two lengths of the pool in his clothes before emerging to
enjoy a beer, while Tom Mulligan inadvertently dived in at
the shallow end, crashing into the pool floor with a sicken-
ing thud – and emerging unscathed. 'Tom is the only fella
who would have got up from that one,' a teammate said.

Dublin's league form in the 2003 campaign was mixed.
Seeking to capitalize on the boom of 2002, the league opener
versus Armagh was fixed for Croke Park, and 51,000 people
saw Dublin annihilated by 1-15 to 0-7 on a bitterly cold February afternoon. The manager angered some within the
squad by insisting afterwards that they had overachieved the
previous season. The remarks brought to a head feelings

within the camp that the Lyons effect was already beginning to wear off.

Dessie Farrell wrote in his autobiography that by 2003 he was 'fed up with his style, fed up with his attitude, fed up with his homespun psychology and fed up with what I perceived to be a flawed approach'. He said the post-match comments after the Armagh thrashing 'rankled with the players, many of whom were already tiring of Lyons's abrasive style'.

Players now speak of a two-tiered structure, with Lyons's cubs such as Alan Brogan and Barry Cahill enjoying tier one status, and the lads over the age of twenty-five stuck firmly in tier two. Lyons was unapologetic from the start when it came to blooding youth and he made it the bedrock of his approach, but some of the older players felt his favouritism marginalized them and split the camp.

Shane Ryan just wanted the same treatment as the likes of Brogan. 'From my perspective, I was twenty-four or twenty-five, not old, but he seemed to treat players of a certain age different to other lads. Anyone who was twenty-two or below, he treated them differently and everyone older got a whole lot of shit off him – including me, who seemed to get it worse, I have no idea why.

'I don't know why he picked on me. Before one match we were in a circle, my chest was unprotected and he's thumping me in the chest, like "Why do I need to do this to motivate you?" and I'm nearly going, "You fucking don't need to do this! Stop hitting me, you're just pissing me off." He says, "I have to light a fire under your arse to do anything," which is completely wrong. Maybe because I was laid back, he had some idea in his head.

'It wasn't just me, he'd pick on other lads like Darren

Homan and Ciaran Whelan. But he'd protect the younger lads and I used to think if he only treated everybody the way he was treating the younger lads we'd be a better team, a stronger team for it. I didn't like being talked to like that.'

Dublin beat Donegal away and Tyrone at home before losing to Kerry in Killarney. They followed that up with defeat at home to Cork and an away win over Roscommon, before another final-day draw with Galway. Over seven league games, the swashbuckling sons of the 2002 summer managed just one goal.

When Farrell spoke of 'homespun psychology', he was perhaps referring to some of Lyons's perceived eccentricities, the ones that had the players in his thrall at the beginning of his tenure but which were beginning to appear jaded just a year later. One key player at that time said on condition of anonymity: 'I felt a lot of his management style, you'd start to see through it a bit after the first year. Instead of encouraging and motivating the lads, they were just getting pissed off and more pissed off, thinking, "This isn't right, we shouldn't be doing this."

'He insisted that you have to have three pints of water before training, and to make sure you did that, on one occasion he wouldn't allow us any water. We're running for an hour and a half and he won't let us have any water. He'd say, "You should have had your three pints." He used to have a phrase, "If it's good enough for Kerry in the '70s it's good enough for you." We're like, "That was in the '70s! That was thirty years ago!"' (Lyons has no recollection of depriving players of water.)

Some of the players were acting as if they'd won an All-Ireland, suffering second-season syndrome. Ray Cosgrove, for one, admits he took his eye off the ball a bit. 'The following season I was a marked man,' he says. 'I still finished our top scorer and had a decent campaign, but no matter what anyone tells you, after the previous season, did I work as hard in 2003 as 2002? Certainly not. I'd be a liar to say I put in the same sort of shift as I did getting to the level I got. That Friday afternoon when you probably went to the gym the year before? Put the feet up now. Another year older, work is in the background, only a spoofer would say my application was the same level. I wouldn't say my performance massively dipped. I was still putting the yards in on the pitch, but it wasn't the same.'

Dublin went into the Leinster championship red-hot favourites for the first time in years, and that tag seemed to fit comfortably when they ruthlessly disposed of Louth in the quarter-finals on 1 June. Cossie, Whelan, Quinn and Bryan Cullen all registered 3 points, Brogan got the goal, and Dublin looked a good bet in what was turning out to be a competitive provincial competition.

Lyons knows he made the biggest mistake of his career for the semi-final. He made wholesale changes for that game against Laois, with an eye on the next match. He drastically underestimated his opponents and he paid the price. Dublin were beaten 0-16 to 0-14, swallowed up by a relentless blue-and-white tide. In Laois's corner was Mick O'Dwyer, the man who carved up Dubs for fun with his '70s and '80s Kerry teams and who ended Kildare's hoodoo against them in the '90s. He infused his supremely gifted team – which boasted Ross Munnelly, Beano McDonald, Pauric Clancy, Tom Kelly and Joe Higgins – with more desire than Dublin could ever muster. Leading by 2 at half-time after playing into the wind, Laois never let up, despite the first-choice players Lyons could spring from the bench. The manager was slaughtered afterwards for starting five players from his own club, Kilmacud Crokes, leaving the likes of Quinn, Sherlock, Goggins, Henry, Farrell and Connell on the bench. Dublin's only shining light on the day was Ballinteer St John's clubman Tom Mulligan, who gave an inspirational display in attack, scoring 3 points. Mulligan would sadly take his own life in 2007, but his contribution to the Dublin cause and his commitment to his county in the difficult 2003 season will never be forgotten.

Dublin kicked sixteen wides to their opponents' six. They were outfought and outplayed, and Lyons knows he was the architect of their downfall. He had the backing of his coaching staff to make the changes he did; but even if he hadn't, he'd have made them anyway. His wasn't management by consensus. 'The biggest mistake I made was trying to get the team ready for an All-Ireland quarter-final because I thought we could win Leinster,' he says now. 'We probably didn't drive hard enough at Laois in that game. I picked a team to try to be ready for a Leinster final.'

One of the Crokes men who came into the team for the Laois game was Liam Óg Ó hEineacháin. 'Liam Óg was a really good player. Every selector picked Liam Óg. The only member that caused any long chat was picking Paul Casey [at wing back]. I was very passionate about him because he gave a lot to us as a team, as a man to go down on the dirty ball, as a man to do the hard yards. He'd been out, and probably in hindsight it was a game too early for him, but that was my loyalty to the young people. And you live and fall. Paul Casey was phenomenal for us in 2002, I'll never forget him going down on the Wexford fella's foot down in Carlow in the last minute, when we won by a point. Paul gave you everything he had, he left nothing on the field. That would have been one of the few in which I pushed hard, but every other decision that day, absolutely everyone was comfortable.'

Lyons's efforts to gee up Ó hEineacháin prior to the game were curious. According to a dressing-room source, when the players huddled together in the warm-up area, Lyons told Ó hEineacháin the worst thing that could happen to him would be to miss some early chances and be taken off at half-time – which was precisely the fate that befell the young forward.

On 28 June Dublin went up to Clones, where they dispatched Derry by 3-9 to 1-9. The Na Fianna trio of Farrell, Sherlock and Connell – all on the bench a fortnight previously – grabbed the goals as Dublin did enough to set up a Round 3 qualifier date with Armagh on 5 July.

Darren Homan had been in and out of the team. Most of his colleagues would have preferred if he was in. He was one of the big-name players left out for the game against Laois and brought back in for the Derry match, in which he excelled. The Ballyboden player often skirted the edge of what was lawful – even on the training ground.

'You're out there representing your family and your club, you're going to do anything you can to win. Everything that was done was done hard. I'm not saying it was always fair, but it was done hard. To the letter of the law, most of the time. But you'd always shake hands afterwards. I'll give you an example: Tom Mulligan and myself were battling to partner Whelan, and I used to bring Tom training. We used to batter each other, now we bashed each other harder than you'd batter someone in inter-county matches. But after training we'd be going home in the same car, we'd shake hands and just get on with it. I tell my son, that's the way it should be. You go hard, but at the end of the day you're both fighting for the jersey and one will get it, you shake and move on.

'At the time, in the A v. B games, if I was on A, Darren Magee was on B, or vice versa. The thing I loved about midfield was you were in direct opposition to the fella going for your jersey. So if you do well on him in training it will be seen, whereas if you're a corner forward you're hoping the corner forward on the other team gets a roasting or the corner back is brutal. You've more of a say in it in midfield. You can go to the manager if the other fella is picked and say, "I'm after roasting him, what's the story there, why is he playing?"'

Homan loved the rough stuff. It was in one of the training matches that he had a coming together with Johnny Magee. The players bounced off each other and Homan adopted a defensive boxing stance. Magee, fearful of what his pal would do to him, got his retaliation in first with a box to the jaw. Other players came in to claw the giants apart, and as they made their way off the pitch, Homan was laughing. "What did you hit me for?" he asked Magee. "Because I wanted to get out of here alive," Magee responded – or words to that effect. It was all par for the course. The Magee brothers came to blows during another heated session and had to be pulled apart by the 5' 9" Jason Sherlock, who swooped in and rugby-tackled Darren to the ground.

It was back to Croker for the third instalment since the previous September of what had become a one-sided rivalry between Dublin and Armagh. A 15 points to 11 defeat kickstarted a series of events that led to a players' revolt.

Keeper Stephen Cluxton was sent off with the game on a knife edge, after taking a heat-of-the-moment swipe at the foot Steven McDonnell. Armagh had Paddy McKeever sent off, but the impact of Cluxton's red on Dublin was much more severe. Johnny Magee was the man who made way for sub goalie Brian Murphy, and from that point on Dublin were shapeless and rudderless.

Magee, once again, felt harshly treated. He had been imperious at centre back until he was called ashore. Once again, it appeared Lyons had been peering into a crystal ball. On the Thursday before the game, a number of senior players received calls from their manager. His message was that he wouldn't be afraid to take big-name players off if things weren't going right. Magee was one of the players who took such a call.

The Armagh match, Magee recalls, was 'the best game I felt I've played in a Dublin jersey. Marking John McEntee, I had a great game, and he didn't have a sniff off me. Clucko did what he did. Next thing my number comes up, I say, "Tommy, what the hell? Who's going on McGeeney, taking the centre back off? You take the corner forward off." "Sit the fuck down," he says to me, and points at the stand. "Go sit in the stand."' Magee and Caffrey had words over the switch in Jury's later that night, which sowed some seeds of discontent between them.

Lyons laid the blame for his team's defeat at his keeper's door, telling the media: 'We can't say they didn't deserve to win, but if Stephen Cluxton did not get sent off we would have won the game.' And: 'It was ridiculous stuff – your goalie getting sent off. It turned the whole game.' He may have been correct in what he said, but the players were livid. Managers weren't supposed to throw their own players under the bus, certainly not in public.

Lyons acknowledges that now, but furiously defends his treatment of a player who would go on to change the way Gaelic football is played. Lyons insists it was he who nurtured

Cluxton and says his reaction to the sending off should not be judged too harshly. 'If I was to do it again I would have chosen the words a little differently, but again when I listen to that, the week after that, I was asked a clear question, do I think the sending off of Stephen Cluxton could have cost us the game and I said it certainly was a significant influence and yes it could.

'I wasn't telling a lie. Do you know what I mean? I wasn't personally blaming Stephen for losing the game but it was a significant event. We had Armagh on the ropes, and it was a very significant event. I'm not saying we would have lost anyhow, but that's the fact of it and you know, if I was doing it again I probably wouldn't even answer the fucking question. But that was me, I never did go out to hurt anybody and I think any player that thought I did hurt them I can say that never was my intention to anybody.

'I still would be able to talk to Stephen Cluxton, we'd slag each other. He really is a top guy. I picked him, Tom Carr dropped him. Davy Byrne fell out with me over Stephen Cluxton, he thought I'd been giving him too much of a chance and not giving Davy a chance to get back. And they're calls you have to make as a manager. Davy is a really nice fella, I was very disappointed when he left the panel. I was just trying to blood a young fella, to give him a bit of match time. For absolute certain our mind wasn't made up about Davy Byrne v. Stephen Cluxton. But Davy wanted more game time. I thought he had enough experience and this fella didn't.

'People talk about his kick-outs. Can I tell you, Stephen Cluxton is as good a shot-stopper as I have ever seen. I remember doing scoring drills on the Saturday before the big games. I had to take him out of the goals at one stage. Forwards would be coming over, "For fuck sake we can't get it past that fella." He was wrecking everyone's confidence! He was a phenomenal shot-stopper, they all talk about his tactical awareness, and that has developed and evolved; but still, pound for pound he's the best shot-stopper in the business.'

That praise was not ringing out in 2003, however. As the players sat in a pub in Carpenterstown, they mulled over the season they'd just had, and most of them were unhappy. Farrell took matters into his own hands and called a meeting in the Burlington Hotel. Only five – Connell, Magee, Cluxton, Sherlock and Farrell himself – turned up. Six more players were outside in cars, fearful of a media stitch-up. The two groups later met up and voted. Paddy Christie voted against ousting the manager, a lone voice among the eleven. The coup petered out, the players no longer united. In his book Farrell insisted that the squad's bond, so tight under Carr, was broken. He wrote: 'We concluded that it was no wonder that we couldn't achieve success on the field if we lacked the stomach off the field as well.'

For Magee, it was past getting personal. He was one of the players who voted to get rid of Lyons, fed up as he was with the perceived victimization. He says: 'Lyons knows what I did that day in Croker, with my cruciate, it could have finished my career. But when you put your career on the line like that, not realizing at the time, when I look on it as a manager, if I had a player like that who is going to give me that kind of heart and determination I'd appreciate him.'

Christie paid the price for his refusal to go along with the heave. He lost friendships. 'I just felt, for me, you always start with yourself,' he explains. 'While [Lyons] shipped a bit of criticism, a lot of fellas had played poorly and I didn't think it made any difference who was manager. I think you should go out and play.

'While the manager definitely has an influence on making a team better or worse, the main element is the player himself, responsibility lies with the player. I felt by all means if you're unhappy go up and have your say either in private or in a group, from elder statesmen, but we had some very poor individual performances.

'Sometimes as well, what I'm always wary of is fellas kicking up a stink and causing trouble when they're not playing. If everyone who wasn't getting his game was to kick up a stink, you're going to have fifteen fellas doing it. So I think, I made a judgement call, I felt the heave was the wrong thing to do.'

Christie's stand impacted on his relationship with other players. 'I'd say there were lads who afterwards didn't look at me in the same light, and I certainly didn't look at them in the same light – the feeling was mutual.' But he didn't let that affect him on the pitch. 'The way I was about things and the way I am to this day is that we're in the business of winning things, and it didn't matter to me who I was playing with. If he was in the right position to get the ball, he got the ball. I never looked at a fella's face to see was it the right guy, it was the jersey I was looking at. If I hated his guts and he hated mine, that didn't matter a fuck to me: I wanted to win.'

The tension in the squad mattered less to Christie than it might have if he had been a drinker. 'I didn't drink, or smoke. I wasn't a social person, so for me it didn't make any difference. I'm sure it would have made a difference for fellas who were very pally with the fellas. The Sunnybank thing wasn't for me. Maybe that made things a little easier.'

In later years, when he had misgivings regarding management, he took a look at himself. 'When I was at the end of my career, I suppose there were different things I would have thought were wrong with the management, that people needed to be got rid of. The first thing I thought was, my time is up, I don't have the heart for it any more. Yes, I could look at getting a new fella, maybe he could revitalize me, but the real problem is me. If you're playing unbelievable football and you're dominating and getting All-Stars every year I think you've probably earned the right to go around dictating things, but for fellas who were playing poorly themselves I thought it was a little bit rich to be giving out about the manager.

'He wasn't the one dropping the ball into the net, he wasn't the one missing scores twenty-one yards out in front of the goals. You start with yourself, and when you have yourself sorted you can start looking around.'

Lyons had no problem staying on following the attempted heave. 'The players who were really driving that meeting were never with me anyhow so that never bothered me at all,' he says. 'It was in double digits, but they didn't make the decision to get me out all the same, therefore they didn't get the room. A lot of the younger players didn't side with them, and the young players are all the players I was picking. I always had the young players, from day one I put a huge amount of energy into them because I felt we had to get seven, eight young players into the team.

'The Whelos and all these lads, if we got enough young players around them it would take the pressure off these guys to plough on. And that was always the strategy. Paddy Christie was a great anchor, you had positions you weren't bothered about, and then you were trying to fill in the boxes.'

Behind the scenes, the manager was angling for a contract extension which he believed would allow him to finish the job he started in 2002. He wanted to infuse the team with the fresh legs he felt Dublin needed to finally regain Sam

Maguire. Had he got the extension he wanted, he would have finished Dessie Farrell's Dublin career. Sherlock too would have been shown the exit door, finally banishing the lingering ghosts of 1995. Lyons believed leading the Dubs to a long-overdue first All-Ireland U-21 title in October 2003 would be enough to convince the county board to prolong his stay. He was wrong.

'I had a meeting with John Bailey in 2003 after winning the 21 All-Ireland and I sat down with him and said, "Now John, we can do two things here, you can either give me an increased term which means I can drive on with more U-21s or if we leave it the way it is I'm gone the end of the year anyhow because I have no mandate to make changes this year." So he came back to me and said no they wouldn't give any extension. They didn't have anyone else in mind at that time. I said I started a project, I committed to bringing on U-21s, and I felt John Bailey dumped on me in the end.

'It was a different dump to Tom. Tom had been there for a good while, there was heroic games against Kerry, but each time Dublin were down, and only when Kerry took the foot off the gas did Dublin come back into it and allow them to be heroic games. Even in the replay they were 12 points down. From that point of view I felt Dublin were a mile away from it. We didn't get them any closer in reality, because unless you win the All-Ireland it doesn't matter when you're bet. You either win it or you don't. That's the way it is.'

Lyons went into 2004 knowing that, no matter what happened, it would be his final season in charge. Despite some moments of positivity, things would only get worse for the team in 2004, and a training trip to Tenerife in April didn't do much to lighten the mood.

Ryan remembers: 'Tommy was a few days late, he flew out late, we were told basically we weren't allowed to do anything. We're there to train, no pints. It wasn't a problem having no pints but when you don't let fellas like that do anything, they'll amuse themselves, so we were in the pool trying to do human pyramids to see how high we could get. Tommy came into the hotel the exact time we were doing it and he flipped it, he lost the plot. We said, "We're bored out of our tits, we have to do something." He didn't relent. A few lads went off anyway. A few went for a few beers.' Some on the panel, as they sat around playing cards on their balconies after a day's work, swear they felt like they were being spied on. It was that kind of trip.

For Johnny Magee it was a struggle just to get on the plane. He had been told to go concentrate on his club football after the Armagh fall-out of the previous summer, and he was fighting to get back in. There were heated phone conversations as the chat kept going back to Armagh and Magee reminded Lyons of his worth. Lyons relented, and the player went to Tenerife.

League form was once again average, mixing a win over Tyrone with defeat to Mayo in a game where Dublin only scored 3 points. Two goals against Longford were the only 3-pointers scored in the entire campaign as they finished fourth behind Tyrone, Kerry and Cork. If the fans weren't yet quite ready to revolt, the county board would struggle to fill the main stand of Parnell Park with fans who still held Lyons in high regard.

Come the Leinster championship quarter-final, come Westmeath – and an embarrassing 0-14 to 0-12 defeat. Dublin cruised through the first half, and led by 3 at the break. But 4 unanswered Westmeath points after the restart exposed the Dubs' soft underbelly. Dublin registered only 3 second-half points into the wind, as Páidí Ó Sé's fired-up men clicked through the gears. Sherlock missed a late goal chance that would have rescued Dublin, but they were dire, and they deserved their fate. The abuse levelled at Lyons at the final whistle was more prolonged, sustained and vitriolic than anything thrown at Mickey Whelan in 1997. He was even spat at as he left the field. Casey says: 'After the Westmeath game, suddenly all the blame was on Lyons. As players, we were getting the backlash. It might have been directed at Tommy, but we were there beside him. It wasn't pretty at all. They were tough times.'

It was back to the qualifiers. The prevailing mood was very dark.

Collie Moran recalls: 'I remember the first back-door game, we were drawn against London. We were getting slaughtered. The talk shows in the evenings, supporters were ringing up, slating the team. It was unbelievable, unprecedented. There was criticism on the streets, no doubt about it. After the Westmeath game there was a famous picture in the paper of Tommy going down the steps to the dressing rooms in the Cusack and a supporter screaming abuse at him while holding his child's hand.

'We had a set time for meeting for games at Parnell Park, we had our routine for league games, but for that London game we met particularly early. Tommy was concerned players would be getting abuse coming in the gates of Parnell, that kind of stuff.'

When Cosgrove's form dipped in 2004, his glorious summer of 2002 became a stick to beat him with, all sacrifices made in the pursuit of glory with Dublin forgotten. 'I got a lot of stick, "You're the one who hit the post", a lot of grief like that. It's part and parcel of it, you get used to it, lads have usually had a few at that stage, so you put them back in their box pretty quickly.

'Even today you meet fellas, they say it and I'm like, was I not the top scorer in the championship? Come back to me when you've managed it. It's humorous but usually you can cut a fella down very quickly, usually with a few pints involved.'

Homan knew the fans were angry, but the buck always stopped with himself. 'When I was playing football for Dublin I was my own worst critic. When you look at yourself in the mirror and you know yourself you were shit, even if everyone says you were great, you know yourself. That's how I always judged my game.'

Others blamed the manager. They needed Lyons to stop talking, to stop whipping up a storm of publicity everywhere he went. He agreed to stop doing interviews, and he believes that made him a target.

'I remember RTÉ news being very aggressive outside the dressing room with me,' he recalls. 'People were making the mistake of treating this like a professional game, whereas it's amateur. I was probably the first fella to get the hairdryer treatment from the media because once you build something, a lot of the players felt I was doing too much of it and felt under pressure so I said OK, and in 2004 I stopped it completely.

'I didn't do any of it. I didn't even do the pre-match interviews for RTÉ, Pillar did them. Therefore that brought RTÉ on top of me. I did that because the players asked me to, people thought it was all about me, but it wasn't about me. I tried to build something and build the confidence levels, and once you did that it was hard to put the genie back in the bottle. But the lads said to me they felt under pressure and I said, "Lads, I'll put a line in the sand," and I didn't do another interview.'

On 12 June, Dublin disposed of London in Parnell Park. On 3 July there was a rare away trip for supporters, who flocked to Carrick-on-Shannon to see Dublin beat Leitrim by 0-13 to 1-4, a trip notable for the gusto with which hundreds of fans broke the fledgling smoking ban in some of the pubs. Dessie Farrell's introduction as sub sparked chants of 'Dessie's gonna get ya' even if he seemed in less than immaculate shape as he hobbled on to the field. In Round 3 of the qualifiers, a week later, there was an easy win over Longford in Portlaoise, 1-17 to 0-11. They followed that up with a 1-14 to 0-13 victory over Roscommon, before they were paired with Kerry in the All-Ireland quarter-final.

On 14 August, Dublin blitzed their old rivals in the first half and should have scored a hatful of goals. But misses by Brogan, Whelan and Sherlock proved costly, robbing the Dubs of the cushion needed in the face of a predictable second-half Kerry onslaught. Kerry's goal, courtesy of skipper Dara Ó Cinnéide in the forty-sixth minute, was one of those that told you to up sticks and get out of there. Colm Cooper's attempt at a point was half blocked, and it came back off the post into the grateful arms of Ó Cinnéide, Dublin's defenders frozen around him. Sherlock's late goal mattered little, and Kerry romped home by 1-15 to 1-8. Brogan, for one, was a shadow of the player that had terrorized defences in 2002. Heads were down, and subs were coming on for the sake of it. On the sideline, the manager knew his time was up.

'Games change very simply. We were well beaten by Kerry, but Gooch was going for a point and Paul Griffin gets half a block on it, and by doing that it hits the post and comes back into Dara Ó Cinnéide's hand,' says Lyons. 'Griff and I would laugh afterwards, "Jesus Christ, if you weren't telling me to *block, block, block* it'd have gone over the bar!" Pillar used to do this blocking training, getting the hand in, and Pillar was brilliant at that stuff. It was his agenda, he drove it. Pillar would have done all of that under me, and he brought it on to another level himself. Games turn on little things. Croke Park is a great stadium, but not a great spot to be when you're bet by 8 points.

'When putting in subs, sometimes you know you're only doing it because if you don't do it they'll all be giving out. You know it won't make any difference at this stage, you know you're gone.'

Moran watched it all from the stands, having suffered what was at one point feared to be a career-threatening injury in a challenge match against Limerick after the London qualifier. The manner of the Kerry defeat was, for him, a defining moment. Players spoke openly about the desire to walk away and live ordinary lives without abuse raining down on them. 'It was the biggest championship defeat I could ever remember for Dublin,' he says. 'I remember sitting there in the subs' seats in the Hogan, arm in a cast and sling, looking down at the corner of Hogan and Canal end and just watching the streams and streams of Dublin fans leaving twenty-five minutes early. That was rock bottom for me.

'They were concerned about my arm and I wasn't sure if I'd ever play again. The squad was on a low. Back then we used to train to the point of exhaustion, and we all questioned was it worth it at all, sacrificing everything and getting nothing but abuse.

'There were no arranged meetings, but individual conversations over a pint in the close season. People were certainly questioning their involvement.'

Lyons knew his time was up, but the players weren't sure who would be leading them into battle in 2005. There was a team meeting at Parnell Park in September. Moran says: 'We all drove into Parnell and didn't know what was going on. He had done a very good job, 2002 he delivered us our first Leinster title and we'll always be grateful for that, a lot of the lads. He'd won an U-21 All-Ireland as manager, so he'd done a lot of good stuff. The team had come to an end. That's not Tommy's fault at all. That meeting was quite sad actually, he sat up the top of the room with his selectors, Dave Billings and Paddy Canning and Pillar and himself, he made the announcement. We all had a bit of a laugh too and shook hands and I suppose that was the end of another era.

'Certainly myself I still have a lot of time for Tommy, good memories and some very bad memories. It wasn't a glory period! But good as well.'

Moran felt Lyons was ultimately quite unlucky how it ended, following a noticeable improvement between 2003 and 2004, but that the manager was beaten in the end by his own game. 'The media love the hype, they enjoyed it back then, but when things go wrong like they did in '03 and '04 it's going to make it worse. If you play up to it as coach or a player when things are going well I think you have to be ready that it's going to be difficult with the media when things go wrong, and that's what happened.'

Homan says: 'Tommy liked the media, loved it when he was winning and they loved him, but when you're losing you're open to criticism, you have to be able to take it. If you're gonna lap up the plaudits you have to listen to the thunder as well.

'The young players coming in, every match was a sell-out, the media attention was huge. For young lads it would have been unnerving. Now Jim Gavin does his stuff with one or two players, you don't really see it any more. Jim is very cute. Tommy was cute at the start, but then to get on well with the media you have to be winning. We were losing at the time. When you lose, the media like to stick it into you as well and I suppose Tommy didn't like that.'

Casey thinks the 2002 Leinster title might have raised too many hopes among the fans. '2002 almost did Tommy more harm than good in the long run. He got us to where expectations from some section of the support went too high too quick. I would have to say he always protected the players as best he could, he knew us young players had a lot of years ahead of us, so did his best for us.'

Magee went on to earn his spurs as a coach and manager. 'I've made a promise to myself that I'd never treat a player the way I had been treated at certain points. I resented it. I want my players to play for themselves, the guy beside him, for their family and friends and clubs, and if I come in on the back of that I'm happy. I played for myself, the guy beside me, friends and family and club. That was my incentive.'

The most prominent managerial face of 2002 would never manage at inter-county level again, although he did flirt with interest from his native county in 2010. As the years passed, he drifted away, out of the public consciousness. He thought from time to time about the injury that curtailed his own playing career, the randomness of it, and how it might have affected the esteem in which he was held. He won a Leinster title at a time when they were hard won, but he walked away a marked man. Tom Carr didn't, yet he retained the support and the affection of the Dublin fans. It was a funny old business.

Lyons says: 'When I used to work with Pat Spillane [on

The Sunday Game], he'd be going on about his eight All-Irelands and nine All-Stars or whatever it was and I'd say, "Pat, how many would you have won if you were born up on the lakes of Leitrim?" Despite him being a great footballer, that's the truth of it. Any player lucky enough to win an All-Ireland is blessed to be playing for the county he's born in. Take Colm O'Rourke, he left Leitrim at ten, he's now a Meath legend, nobody ever talks about him being from Leitrim.

'I left Mayo at ten, they still talk about me being a Mayo man. Because I didn't achieve on the pitch. I did a cruciate in 1979 and they didn't know what it was. I was on the minor squad that year, and got an injury. It's gas how things work out in life. I was sitting in the house and a friend of mine rings. He says, "Tommy, we need a goalie to come play for Wayside Celtic." I arrived up to play and the goalie had turned up but the centre forward didn't. "Go up and play centre forward." I played little or no soccer bar out in the field with the neighbours. A ball came over the top and I got to it before the goalie and the goalie's studs went straight into my stomach, severing my intestines.

'I was out for twelve months, had major surgery. It shows you how life can change. That was Easter, I had been on the Dublin squad, we'd only done two or three sessions. In those times they weren't preparing in December. And that finished me. I played for Kilmacud Crokes all the way through but only on one leg. I was finished at nineteen.'

Lyons remains a friend of Dublin football. He's a businessman who can still be called on to help in the background when required. For him, it's still about that jersey, the one he fought for and continues to fight for, away from the spotlight. 'As far as I'm concerned, I went in to do a job. I carried the baton for three years, I think I passed the baton on with the thing in a better place from when I took the job on, that's all anyone can really do,' he says. 'You're only ever carrying the baton when managing county teams and anyone who thinks any different is only kidding themselves.

'If I achieved anything, I created a togetherness. Under-21s, lads coming into the panel, this is about everybody, not any one person. Everybody tries to do it their own way. I'm still very happy with my track record as a manager, all the jobs that I've done.

'I left an awful lot of players in a better space than when I first came across them. And I absolutely have to acknowledge there will always be some players who thought I was over hard on them, and that's just the way it is.'

8. The Circle

The search for a successor to Tommy Lyons took more than three months and was marked as usual by suspicion, indecision and farce.

Whenever a vacancy arose, the name of Brian Mullins was invariably mentioned. The St Vincent's clubman was one of the greatest players to ever pull on a jersey. He claimed his fourth All-Ireland in 1983 after a near-fatal car accident had put him out for the guts of two years. He returned a shadow of the gargantuan player he had been, but driven by a ferocious desire that more than made up for the physical decline.

Shortly after Lyons quit, Mullins met with the county board to discuss taking over. He was forceful, perhaps too forceful. He outlined a vision for Dublin football that might have spooked some of the decision-makers. Mullins waited for three months to sign the papers, the same length of time he'd spent in hospital in early 1981 recovering from a shattered leg. While Mullins waited, John Bailey approached Mick O'Dwyer, meeting the Kerry legend in the K Club Hotel to offer him the job. O'Dwyer, at that time the manager of Laois, accepted the invitation and plans were in place to establish his backroom team. News of his impending appointment leaked, and when the reaction made it apparent that he would forever be working against tradition and the intolerance of former players, he turned it down. In a time of mixed messages and communication problems, Mullins's demand that Dublin's media affairs be handled by a PR firm was quite apt.

Paul 'Pillar' Caffrey was a man who operated largely in the shadows of the inter-county scene. He had played a bit with Dublin in the 1980s but was best known at the end of 2004 as the garda JLO (junior liaison officer) who had led his club Na Fianna to an All-Ireland club final in 2000 and for his cameo as boss in 2002 when Tommy Lyons suffered his health scare before the All-Ireland quarter-final against Donegal. Caffrey had been an able assistant to Lyons, working largely on Dublin's defensive drills, quietly and efficiently in the manner of a coach who knew his place in the pecking order.

In November 2004, following O'Dwyer's rebuff, Pillar was invited to put together his team to take Dublin forward. It was, after the dalliance with Micko, a conservative appointment. Some of the squad were consulted – unofficially – prior to the appointment, and were thought to be lukewarm at best. He had worked with those players for three mixed years, had watched his relationship with the Na Fianna players deteriorate somewhat in and around 2003 when they felt he wasn't pushing their cause for selection. But it took just one meeting for him to change the minds of the squad.

'Funny, when I heard Pillar got the job, myself anyway and a lot of the lads thought, "Aw, for Jesus' sake, this is going to be the same again now,"' says Shane Ryan. 'He was doing his job as a selector and backing up Tommy in everything. But once we had our very first meeting the first night and Pillar gave his spiel, we all thought, "This is brilliant! This is going to be completely different." We never saw any of that when he was a selector.

'As I understand it, from talking to different people,

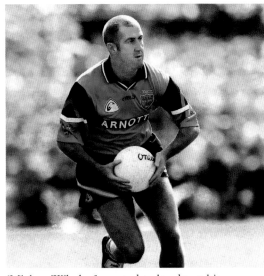

'Mickey [Whelan] wanted to lay down his marker . . . he told me I was burned out and needed a break, even though I felt the contrary' —Paul Clarke. (David Maher / Sportsfile)

'If people did come in after '95, and they have a view of it being an unwelcoming dressing room, and if I was being particularly unwelcoming to them, I fully accept their view. I cannot dispute or deny it'—Keith Barr. (Ray McManus / Sportsfile)

The Dublin team for the first game of the 1997 championship, against Meath, included 12 starters from the 1995 final. They came almost all the way back from a huge first-half deficit, but Paul Bealin's last-minute penalty hit the crossbar. (Ray McManus / Sportsfile)

'I was an army officer, I had dealt with people all along. It's not as if I needed training in dealing with people'— Tommy Carr (pictured with County Board chairman John Bailey and selector Dom Twomey at the announcement of Carr's appointment as manager in December 1997). (David Maher / Sportsfile)

The huddle before Carr's first championship game as manager, against Kildare. Future Dublin manager Jim Gavin – known to some teammates as 'Champo Jim', as they perceived him to be a management favourite – can be seen tying his bootlace. (David Maher / Sportsfile)

'If some of these fucking clowns thought they were great because they won one All-Ireland, well then shame on them' —Eamon Heery, who came back into the squad after missing the All-Ireland season (pictured here against Kildare in 1998).
(David Maher / Sportsfile)

'I think there was a feeling in Dublin that Crokes lads weren't really Dublin lads'— Mick O'Keeffe (pictured after scoring against Louth in 1999).
(Brendan Moran / Sportsfile)

A heaving Hill 16 in 1999, before the refurbishment of Croke Park.
(Aoife Rice / Sportsfile)

Carr is ordered from the pitch by referee Michael Daly after aiming verbals at Kerry's Maurice Fitzgerald – who then nailed an astounding sideline ball to win the 2001 All-Ireland quarter-final. (Ray McManus / Sportsfile)

'I won Man of the Match that day, but I will always be remembered for hitting the post'— Ray Cosgrove, whose magical summer of 2002 ended when he missed a relatively straightforward free in the last minute against Armagh in the All-Ireland semi-final. (Brian Lawless / Sportsfile)

Dublin supporters turn their anger on manager Tommy Lyons after a Leinster championship defeat to Westmeath in 2004. (David Maher / Sportsfile)

Next up for Dublin was London, in the qualifiers. Some fans in Parnell Park came out in support of Lyons. (Ray McManus / Sportsfile)

'Croke Park is a great stadium, but not a great spot to be when you're bet by 8 points'—Tommy Lyons on the 2004 All-Ireland quarter-final defeat to Kerry. (Matt Browne / Sportsfile)

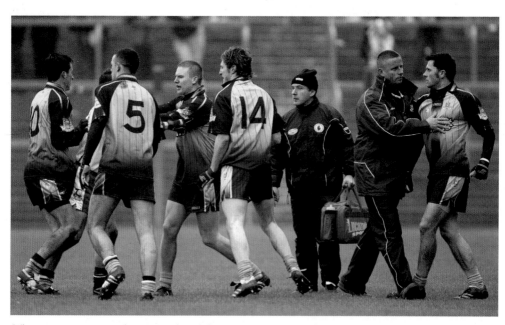

'There was an atmosphere people might say wasn't pretty, but as a sportsman playing in that game, they're the games you want to play in'—Paul Casey on the 'Battle of Omagh' in February 2006, which saw four red cards and nine yellows – and a Dublin victory. (Oliver McVeigh / Sportsfile)

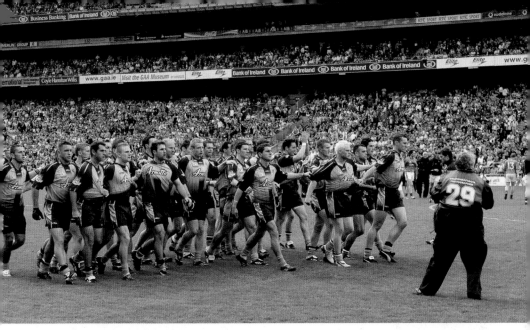

Dublin's ceremonial march to Hill 16 – a feature of the 2006 championship – was disrupted when Mayo decided to warm up in that end of the pitch before the All-Ireland semi-final. Dublin lost after blowing a six-point lead. (Damien Eagers / Sportsfile)

'The worst thing is my mum worked with Rooney's wife!'—Mark Vaughan, who aimed a 'Texas Longhorn' gesture at Laois defender Darren Rooney after scoring a goal against Laois in the 2007 championship. (Ray McManus / Sportsfile)

Pat Gilroy (right) and trainer Mickey Whelan, who took over after the 2008 season and put the Dubs on the road to the All-Ireland. (Brian Lawless / Sportsfile)

The end of the chaos years: Stephen Cluxton lines up the free that would beat Kerry in the 2011 All-Ireland final. (Brian Lawless / Sportsfile)

nobody was really given any say when Lyons was manager, so dissenting voices might not have been tolerated. Everything completely changed when Pillar took over. He probably disagreed with a lot of what Tommy did but couldn't say it. Maybe he did say it and got ignored. But his whole approach, you wanted to do everything he was saying, this was really good, everyone was coming out thinking, "This is real. We could make a real shot of something with this team."'

The versatile Ryan was rejuvenated by the new boss, thrust into a midfield role that would redefine how Dublin played. The Naomh Mearnóg man had played in all defensive positions and in the half forwards, but it was at midfield under Caffrey that he would play his best football for Dublin. He developed an almost telepathic relationship with Cluxton, who was becoming increasingly accurate with his long, diagonal kick-outs. The nimble Ryan's job was to widen the pitch, and he would mop up a huge amount of ball direct from his keeper's deliveries.

Moran, who had contemplated throwing in the towel earlier that year, was blown away by the philosopher who had been hanging around all those years, his true self hidden from view. 'It really was an amazing time when I look back on it, those couple of years under Pillar,' he recalls.

'We had a very memorable meeting the first night in DCU. At that stage, when he took over, the confidence of the squad was on the floor. We were all just sitting there looking at our shoes, not able to look at him and not able to look at ourselves and each other, it was a real low, but he did a fantastic job in building the squad back up, putting in a value system and trying to get a bit of pride back in the squad. He wanted us to be hard to beat, get the building blocks right and bring back the buzz.'

Caffrey had an unusually big backroom team. Dave Billings was a selector and also handled logistics. The other selectors were Galway legend Brian Talty – whose head got in the way of Mullins's elbow in that 1983 All-Ireland final, causing Mullins to be sent off – and Kieran Duff, who achieved infamy in the same game when he was dismissed for kicking an opponent as he lay on the ground. The defence coach was the formidable Ski Wade, and ex-League of Ireland stopper Gary Matthews was the goalkeeping coach. Ray Boyne compiled the match-day statistics, DCU's Niall Moyna assisted with strength and conditioning, and Dr Gerry McElvaney headed the medical team. Paul Clarke was back as a trusted lieutenant and physical trainer.

Pillar's revolution extended to every facet of an organization that saw Dublin transformed into a set-up bordering on professional. The players' every coaching and dietary need was catered for, and Caffrey always found a sympathetic ear on the county board if he needed any additional funding. Given the resources at his disposal, winning one Leinster title in seven years was no longer an option. He had to deliver.

Caffrey, who would become something of an orator, swore by team meetings, where the squad would dissect the action on DVDs. They were routinely divided into groups and asked to thrash out ideas, much like corporate employees might be on a HR away-day. A psychologist, Dave Whelan, delivered sermons for the mind. Each player was given his own personalized season plan, with key performance indicators (KPIs) to abide by. Organizationally, nothing was left to chance. Each player's timetable was mapped out on a sheet, and they knew in advance what Clarky's training would involve. Players were also requested to pen a match report after the championship games, and at the end of each season they would sit down with management for their review.

Whereas Lyons was all about the hard yards, with Caffrey it was the inches.

The new philosophical and motivational approach manifested in the infamous Blue Book, a manual produced by Caffrey to inspire his troops. Many of the players from that time still have their copy of the book. The Blue Book was a sort of customized diary, small enough to be carried around in a kitbag, but big on ideals. In his memoir *Dub Sub Confidential*, reserve keeper John Leonard describes the book as containing quotes – including one on the inside front cover from World War II US General George Patton which the 'warriors' were asked to recite in pairs before training. The Blue Book was not under any circumstances to be shown to anyone outside the Dublin camp.

Caffrey took the little book very seriously. 'He spoke of special places, special people and the desire to be a success,' Leonard writes. 'He spoke of the transient nature of the game, of sacrifice and of commitment. He called each one of us by name and hand-delivered the sacred tome to us.' The book evolved from season to season, and some of the words it contained were contributed by the players themselves during their corporate training-style meetings.

Much of what Pillar was doing with Dublin was an attempt to draw on the success of the Ulster teams. 'I got a couple of blue books, and we completely bought into it,' says Ray Cosgrove. 'It was something Pillar had learned from McGeeney and Armagh, the close-knit environment they were working under, what was expected from them. They were winning Ulster championships, and were a lot further along the track than this Dublin team, so we bought into it. If we wanted to progress and deliver an All-Ireland, these were the added bits we had to go through, these were the standards expected.' If partnering up to read quotes before going out on the pitch was what was required, then so be it.

'I learned myself, when I was fortunate to work with Pillar, that you give your heart and soul for the group of players,' Clarke says. 'You provide everything for them, tick all the boxes for them, facilitate them, you make sure everything is in place for them to perform. You set the highest standards you can, so on match day they can do their business.'

The team moved much of their operation to DCU in Glasnevin. 'We came in and set up close links with the likes of Niall Moyna in DCU to try and change the training methods and habits,' Clarke says. 'The idea of go out and do a 10,000-metre run or twenty laps of the pitch was gone. As the season went on, running time was reduced, recovery comes in, so when you reached championship you had the balance. We replicated what was going on in matches. So in August you're not doing ten 200-metre runs. There'll be odd times fellas would say we're not doing enough and you might throw in a gut buster, but not the week of a championship game.

'We had the best training facilities, the best of physios and medics on call. If someone picked up an injury they would be in hospital straight away being treated. Eating for us in the '90s was tea and biscuits. You wouldn't see a sandwich in training, you knew if you did there must be a championship match coming up. We got a chocolate biscuit! Under Pillar we were going to the Goblet pub [in Artane], eating fish, beef or chicken, being fed properly. Gear was organized, we had winter and summer gear for training and playing. I was organizing gym membership, doing deals with Total Fitness at the time, getting DCU membership for the lads so they could go and do their gym work.'

By the time the players had listened to philosophical musings, read their piece for the day, analysed opponents, absorbed the positive messages stuck up on the dressing-room walls, tuned their mindset to positive, done training and eaten the dinner afterwards, four and a half hours might have passed.

Paul Casey loved it. 'It was a totally different regime and [Caffrey] made that clear from the very start. We were there to work hard, it was serious work, you weren't there for the ride, it was to put it in and for Dublin to be successful, and it was going to take a lot of hard work.

'That was clear early on. The players all enjoyed it, they were very enthused by the set-up and everybody was pulling in the one direction, which wasn't the case towards the end of Lyons's time. Pillar glued the whole thing together and got them all moving in the one direction.'

After another average league campaign, with four wins and three defeats, Dublin regained their Leinster crown in 2005. In the first round against Longford, Conal Keaney and Alan Brogan registered 2-7 between them, while Mossy Quinn contributed with 5 points. On 5 June they overcame Meath by 1-12 to 1-10, Brogan top-scoring with 1-3. New arrival Mark Vaughan got two frees. Almost 66,000 were in Croke Park to see Stephen O'Shaughnessy enjoy an outstanding debut at the back, Dublin recovering from an early Graham Geraghty goal to put another one over on their old rivals. Ciaran Whelan left his mark on Nigel Crawford.

A fortnight later, Wexford were Dublin's opponents in the Leinster semi-final.

'In Wexford terms, we were a serious team,' recalls Wexford forward John Hegarty. 'We were coming in with a very different mindset and we expected to beat Dublin because they hadn't featured in the league which we had gotten to the final of. It was all going well, everything we'd intended to do was on track. We got a goal halfway through the second half. What followed is probably the last time it happened until recently: Cluxton looked rattled. He took two poor kick-outs just afterwards. I thought "This doesn't happen, we have them here."

'That was one of the times we came up against Dublin and thought, "Yes, we have these rattled." Guys like Cosgrove, Vaughan and Mossy you thought you could really get at. You could certainly distract them from the game. Cluxton was coming with a rep he could lose the head and wasn't the influence he would become, but he was a respected keeper.

'They had a few guys who played on the edge. Prime example was Ciaran Whelan. He had at that point got a number of sendings-off. He was their talisman, also somebody we felt we could get at. I felt he responded to somebody trying to get at him but he got away with it sometimes.'

Opponents in those days knew that hitting Whelan was a waste of time, unless the player doing the hitting was strong enough to make it count. Wexford had a man who could take or leave the ball. Midfielder Nicky Lambert, hard as nails, had one job. Watch Whelan, and if he got a chance to nail him, then nail him.

'When Nicky was hurling, he was full forward and his only job was to run at the goalie every chance he got,' explains Hegarty. 'A Limerick lad said one time that "Every time the ball went over the bar he slapped me in the goal and pulled on the crossbar." He was a really good athlete, strong, but didn't have a great football brain.

'His job against Kildare in a previous game was to look after Dermot Earley. This was one of his first assignments, I don't know what happened but halfway through the first half Earley was stretchered off the pitch with a bad injury. We said, "Nicky, what the fuck did you do like, that's over and above." His kinda attitude was "You told me to stop him." So we had to tone it down a bit. We had to put the brakes on him a little bit as he was half mental.'

Hegarty had played for Wexford against Dublin in the 2000 championship when his day-tripping side, with nothing in mind except to enjoy the occasion at HQ, were steamrollered by Carr's Dublin team. He also togged out in 2002, when Casey saved the day for Dublin. If that unheralded Wexford team had designs on beating the Dubs, this one was certain it could. Rattling Whelan and Cluxton was one component, keeping the crowd quiet was another.

'What I would also have felt, going back to 2000 when we played them in Croke Park, the crowd were never a factor because it wasn't competitive. When they became competitive, especially in 2005, the crowd were certainly a factor.

'When I say Cluxton was rattled, it wasn't just that he was rattled, it was the fact the crowd had gone quiet. All of a sudden when they got the goal [by Jason Sherlock] the whole place erupted. It was the first time playing Dublin in Croker that you kind of said the crowd actually is a factor. We never noticed it before.'

After Sherlock's goal, the Dubs held on to win by 4 points. But all was not well. Hegarty had a front-row view of Dublin's organizational problems on the pitch. Dublin's leaders were swallowed up by the occasion. Blue Books tucked away in the gear bags, there were no cool heads.

'I think when things turned against them, they didn't have

a default fall-back position that they now have, to say, "Look, lads, we need to shore it up for the next five minutes." Everybody was looking from one to the other, "What do we do now?" When the game then swung in their favour again, it was as much a relief to the players as the crowd, oh thank fuck, everything is back to normal, it's all OK again, without them actually having a process to get back to that point.

'They were quite brittle. Mark Vaughan was so easy to get at. Absolutely the same with Mossy. Even maybe more so than Mark, when Mossy's frees went, his general play went as well.'

In the Leinster final, against Laois, the Dubs were 2 down with seven minutes remaining, time and the weight of recent history against them. But Mossy Quinn, much maligned by opponents, refused to wilt under pressure. After missing some scoreable frees earlier on, he kicked over a sixty-ninth-minute dead ball from forty-three metres to level the game. In injury time, he popped over a 45 to win it – prompting thousands of delirious fans to invade the Croke Park pitch in an outpouring of joy not seen for three years.

'There was this great sense that Dublin were on the verge of something big, of an All-Ireland,' Moran recalls. 'It was a great time as well in the province, Westmeath and Laois felt they had done it before in Leinster and could do it again, Kildare and Meath were always there. Wexford had a tidy team as well with Redmond Barry and Mattie Forde – they were doing damage in the league and the back door over a couple of seasons, taking big scalps, a proper team. The 2005 win over Laois was a huge moment for us, particularly after such a painful '03 and '04 and the dramatic fashion of coming from 2 points behind.'

Under Pillar, the lads who worked as hard as they did were

permitted to play hard when the occasion called for it. The semi-final win over Wexford was good enough reason to go out, with the final against Laois almost a month away. What else would an emerging inter-county force do after a win over a minnow, other than embark on a two-day bender? Moran recalls: 'The celebrations Sunday would turn into Monday. Back to the Sunnybank after the game, right in the midst of all the fans and that kind of stuff, and on to Coppers.

'Then the next day out for a bit of golf and a few more pints and a bit of craic. It was great. That summer, we used to go out golfing on the Monday to Hollystown, who were always great to us. One day, I came home from the golf at 6 p.m. and left the lads out there – they were still having pints. I was tired from the game, we had played Wexford in the semi-final and I was thinking ahead to the training. We had a hard night on the Sunday and I'd made my mind up I was going to bed.

'I was getting texts from Jayo and a few of the other lads: "Come on, we're going out", but I went to bed and thought that was going to be it. I was still living with my mum and dad at the time. In the middle of the night there was some banging, my parents woke up and my ma was terrified we were being burgled. The banging kept going, my dad went downstairs, I was crawling out the bed at that stage, I just heard the door open and my mother screaming down the stairs, "Don't go out in case he's jumped on," and then heard the front door opening and all I heard from downstairs was "Ah Jayo how are ya?"

'So five of the lads ran up the stairs, into the bedroom, picked me up in my boxer shorts, carried me down to outside, where they'd somehow got a big bus, the Vengabus! So they threw me on to the coach and handed me a bottle of beer and then all went back inside, produced a pair of my tracksuit bottoms and runners. So we went to everyone's house that wasn't there, we went to Ray Cosgrove's, and Coman Goggins', one by one picked them up and made it in to Coppers. I'm not sure if Jim Gavin would like that! Good times.'

On a quiet day in the Sunnybank Hotel in Glasnevin, it wouldn't be unusual for All-Ireland winners to make up the bulk of the clientele. It was an old-school boozer, a long puc from Croker. It was in the Sunnybank that Dublin legend John McCarthy was asked, following a Dublin draw with Louth in the Leinster championship in 1973, to put down the jar and come play for his county. Put down the jar he happily did, and made his debut in the replay. '73 was of course a bad year for the Dubs, and it wasn't until another Sunnybank stalwart – Jimmy Keaveney – made his return the following year that Heffo's Army began to march. Keaveney's old mate Paddy Cullen was another regular visitor, and in 2004 filmed a documentary, *Dublin in the Rare Ould Times*, with actor Colm Meaney in the lounge, with a large crowd of locals watching on from behind the cameras. When they were told to shut up, they shut up, and when the director yelled cut, orders for more scoops flooded in. Once back on standby, the crowd obediently shut up once more, refusing to take a sip unless given permission.

Until Tommy Carr's time as Dublin manager, the Sunnybank was considered more of a 'country' GAA establishment. Tipperary superstar John Doyle, one of the greatest hurlers of all time, would often sup away unnoticed by regulars, as would '80s Galway hard man Brendan Lynskey, while Cork hero Billy Morgan was also in.

Carr liked the idea of keeping the squad together after the big games instead of letting them go their separate ways immediately afterwards. Gradually it became the custom to go en masse to the Sunnybank. The players would dine on the buffet in the Chinese restaurant upstairs, then march down for pints. In those days before formal county tracksuits, the players wore civvies, which posed a problem for some bar staff who found it difficult to spot who was a player drinking off the tab and who was a fan chancing his arm. Many patrons walking through the middle lounge in those days would spot the ragtag bunch of lads drinking together, assume they were on a stag party and jog on. Vinnie Murphy in particular is remembered as the joker in the pack, tearing strips out his colleagues and anyone who lingered a moment too long in their presence – including the bar staff.

Tommy Lyons put an end to the Sunnybank ritual, preferring to take his players for a sitdown meal somewhere more respectable. Bertie Ahern got involved in brokering deals with hotels to feed the Dubs, helping to strike an arrangement with Jury's 'on the cheap'. But Pillar Caffrey had built up a relationship with the Sunnybank's owner, the late Peter Garvey, while managing the local Na Fianna club, and he brought his custom back as soon as he had the chance.

The Dubs were eventually given their own backroom VIP area for post-match drinks, before spilling out into the main lounge, where they would be joined by thousands of fans queuing eight deep at the bar. The bar staff were thrilled to see Pillar's players in their special t-shirts, knowing then exactly who was on the tab. Ahern would sup a pint with the team before fleeing, unmolested, out the fire escape. The fans would fall over themselves to get autographs with players who'd never won an All-Ireland, despite the fact they might have been sitting at the bar beside an unassuming oul' fella with three in his back pocket.

*

Caffrey was determined not to fix anything he deemed un-
broken. The Dublin team that took to the field for the quarter-
final with Tyrone on 13 August was pretty much the same as
every other team he picked, and Pillar repeated the dose for
the replay after that first game was drawn. It meant that he
made only a single alteration to his starting fifteen across the
entire championship: Vaughan for Sherlock against Wexford.
It was difficult for the substitutes who knew they wouldn't be
playing, barring a catastrophe. One of the elements of Pillar's
ritual was to take only the starting players for a pre-match
gee-up.

On forty-nine minutes, with Tyrone trailing by three,
Owen Mulligan left Paddy Christie on his back some forty-
five yards from goal, turned towards the Canal End and ran.
He dummied to fist past Stephen O'Shaughnessy, and the
young tyro bought it. Advancing further, he feigned to lay
off past Casey. Another man down. With Cluxton to beat,
Mulligan ignored his old mentor Peter Canavan and stuck it
into the roof of the net. Scores level.

With sixty-nine minutes on the clock, Tyrone were up by
2. Mossy Quinn pulled one back, and then in stoppage time
had a kick towards the Hill to equalize. It was straight in
front of the posts, but forty-five yards out and missable.
Some mouthing from Tyrone defenders was deemed enough
to bring the ball forward, and the St Vincent's man levelled
it at 1-14 apiece.

In the replay a fortnight later, everything that was infuri-
ating about Dublin resurfaced, and Mossy endured one of
his untimely off-days. Mulligan, who had been out of form
until his wonder goal, scored 1-7 – including a goal in front
of Hill 16 that killed off a second-half Dublin revival. He
marked what was effectively the match winner with a puffing

of the chest in front of people who would in time appreciate his genius.

After Dublin were drawn against Longford in the first round of the 2006 Leinster championship, Longford County Chairman Martin Skelly approached the Leinster Council and suggested playing the game on his patch. He was told that, provided he got the ground up to scratch on time, he had a deal. Local businesses clubbed together to raise €130,000, with the rest of the €250,000 put up by the Council, Croke Park and the Lotto. The result was a new main pitch, new seats adjacent to the stand, and an occasion that is still talked about. Treasurer Brendan Gilmore hailed the 'fantastic' travelling support, insisting he wouldn't see its like again in his lifetime.

He almost witnessed the result of a lifetime. Dublin – who had beaten Longford by 19 points the previous season – were poor, and thankful for a Vaughan goal that helped them to a 1-12 to 0-13 win in front of 16,000 fans. Conal Keaney kicked over 8 points on a gloriously sunny day, but few of his colleagues ever got going. During a pit stop for pints on the way home – in a pub only recently acquired by Sunnybank owner Peter Garvey – a naked Vaughan jumped into a lake. He had everyone in stitches – except perhaps Pillar, who would drop him for the next match.

It was back to HQ for the Leinster semi-final on 25 June. Dublin's 3-17 to 0-12 win over Laois brought back the swagger, introducing a new Dublin to an expectant audience. It was marked down as the performance of a generation, young thoroughbreds putting their rivals to the sword. Laois were a team at the pinnacle of their powers, but couldn't live with Caffrey's men. Cossie was back, and the Hill rocked as he registered 1-3, joined on the scoresheet by Quinn (1-4), substitute Vaughan (1-0) and the ever-impressive Keaney (0-5). Laois's entire half forward line was withdrawn, and manager Micko – who could have been sitting in Dublin's dugout – humiliated.

That match also saw the debut of a pre-match ritual that quickly became infamous: the Hill 16 salute. No other team could count on such a sheer volume of backing from the stands, and nothing could compare to Hill 16 in full voice. Pillar wanted to maximize its effect.

John Leonard describes its introduction in his book: '[Caffrey] wanted to add a new element to our pre-match ritual. Each of us was to grab a teammate by the shoulder as we jogged around the pitch during the training warm-up . . . after the pre-match team photograph in the centre of the Croke Park pitch, we would jog down slowly to the Hill in this manner, presenting a united front. We were to soak up the atmosphere of Croker. We were to encourage the Hill and the noise. The idea was to absorb that energy, noise and fervour collectively for a short few seconds.'

'Pillar was a massive Dublin fan, first and foremost,' says Ray Cosgrove. 'So he asked us to soak it up, embrace it, and to show the fans we respected them and were in it together. He would say things like "The circle is only as strong as the weakest link", or "The unit is strongest as a whole". So we were brothers in arms, hands on shoulders, enjoying our bond with Hill 16. And to be honest, the players loved it. There were thirty of us, united as a group, fighting together.

'You didn't want to take it for granted. I embraced it, it was like giving something back. It was novel, because no other team had a Hill 16 to salute, but whether it gave us an edge or not I don't know.'

Another player recalls: 'It became a bit of an in-house joke the longer it went on. What are we doing here? I saw a couple of lads with their heads down one day, struggling to stop laughing.'

In the Leinster final, the Offaly of Ciaran McManus, Niall McNamee and Karol Slattery were no match for a rampant Dublin, and eased to a 1-15 to 0-9 defeat on 16 July in front of a spectacular crowd of almost 82,000. It was a procession. The crowd lapped it up. The players then embarked on another of their two-day sessions, beginning naturally in the Sunnybank. As shadows grew longer, the Delaney Cup was passed around the car park by supporters, nobody quite sure who was supposed to be looking after it. Anyone foolish enough to park there had their cars used as beer mats. If they tried to leave, they were told to get out of it, get up the yard or get another pint into them. Above, in one of the bed-rooms, an English tourist who had booked in for a quiet night's rest before he got home was looking down at the hordes, wondering what the hell he'd gotten himself into.

A Coppers lock-in was followed up by a round of golf and another stop on Harcourt Street. Life as a Dub was fun, but even an often-forgiving Caffrey felt obliged to read the riot act after that particular bender, warning about the dangers of drinking to excess.

Dublin made short work of Westmeath in the All-Ireland quarter-final, winning 1-12 to 0-5. The win set up a semi-final clash with Mayo, who were being given little chance, on 27 August.

As they prepared to head out to the pitch, Dublin's players got word that the Mayo players were warming up at the Hill 16 end. They assumed – as did the RTÉ commentators – that it was an intentional provocation. The Dubs would have to warm up at the other end and forgo the Hill salute; or else they'd have to march through the Mayo players and then warm up alongside them.

'I don't think it was Mickey Moran who instigated it,' reckons Ray Cosgrove. (TV footage appeared to show Moran unsuccessfully urging his players to move to the Canal end.) 'It was David Brady and a couple of other lads spontaneously leading the charge.'

The Dubs emerged from the tunnel and made their way to the bench in front of the Cusack Stand for the team photo. After the photo, Cosgrove says, 'We weren't going to deviate from our warm-up plans, so we headed off to the Hill as usual.' Ciaran Whelan, furiously determined to get to the Hill, had to be held back by the jersey just enough so he wouldn't sprint off on his own. With just fifteen minutes to go to throw in of the All-Ireland semi-final, scores of bodies became entangled as both sides refused to budge from the Hill 16 half of the pitch.

'We did our usual drills, and I was warming up with Goggsy [Coman Goggins], doing a few blocks, when I looked up and the female Mayo physio was lamped with a 40-yard cross-field pass,' says Cosgrove. 'She was cleaned out, and fell like a bowling pin.' A contrite Alan Brogan could only apologize for one of his few wayward passes. Caffrey smashed into the back of Mayo selector John Morrison, and opposing players started mouthing at each other. The fans lapped it up. Mayo had been waiting since 1951 to win the All-Ireland: they were at least as desperate for success as their city-slicker rivals.

It took 17 minutes for Dublin, so often the fastest out of the blocks, to register their first point. Mossy Quinn was misfiring, and at the other end Ciarán McDonald was in the mood. Keaney's score to make it 0-1 to 0-4 should have settled Dublin down, but within minutes Whelan was blessed to escape a sending-off for poleaxing Ronan McGarrity, who would later be forced out of the game by the impact of the thump. (The remorseful Dub apologized the following day, the Mayo man graciously accepting.) Another few wides into the Hill 16 end robbed the Dubs of momentum temporarily, but following a Keaney goal and a point from Cossie they were in front. Sherlock rattled the bar and Brogan came close, but they went in at half-time a point down. Shortly after half-time, Jayo scored a goal, and Brogan reeled off 3 unanswered points. Dublin were purring and Mayo's first point of the second half was only enough to reduce their deficit to 5. With forty-six minutes on the clock, Dublin were up by 7 and Mayo, clinging on for dear life, sprang Andy Moran. He goaled immediately. It was his first ever in the championship, and the first Dublin had conceded all summer.

With fifty-five minutes on the clock, the sides were level. Two minutes later, Conor Mortimer chipped one over and Dublin were behind. Hill 16, so belligerent until that point, was stunned temporarily into silence. Not again, please, this can't happen again. The players, minds blank, bodies aching, looked to one another for answers. Those answers, crafted over time by heartache and despair, lay within. Pillar pleaded for one last push. This was where the inches counted. This was where they would summon the spirit from all their vast reserves of courage. General Patton's words were supposed to echo now. Remember the sacrifices.

They had ten minutes to make it count, and the seconds seemed to be evaporating. With three minutes to go, Brogan nailed an equalizer into the canal end. The Hill erupted. That was the hard part done, surely. Vaughan kicked a huge one from distance, but it careered back off the post. McDonald, who in the first half struck a Maurice Fitzgerald-esque beauty over the bar, then found space in a crowded phone box to curl over an impossible point. With seventy minutes on the clock and Mayo in the lead by 1, Vaughan stepped up to take a 45 close to Hogan Stand sideline. He hit the crossbar.

The players fought like hungry dogs for scraps from the master's table. Any possession would do for Dublin. Another late free. This time from fifty yards, Vaughan again missed it. Mayo's triumphant support greeted the final whistle like it was 1951. Dublin were out yet again. That the match had been a modern classic was irrelevant.

'I remember coming off the pitch and, 6 up, Pillar gave me a high five,' recalls Cosgrove. 'It was basically, "Bang, here we go, we're getting to the Holy Grail now, the boys will close it out, we'll march on to the third Sunday in September."

'But by the time I'd walked up the steps to take my seat on the bench, fucking Andy Moran had got the goal.

'So the lead became 3, and the tide had simply turned. They just kept coming and coming at us, they couldn't stop the onslaught. Ciarán McDonald kicked the winner that day. From a winning position, in my opinion, whatever about '02 and me hitting the post, I felt we were a young team that didn't believe, there was no talk of winning All-Irelands in '02. We were only seeing how far we could go, but we didn't believe that we were as good as Kerry or Armagh at that stage. That's being very honest. In '06 we had matured as a team, developed physically, were more competitive, from the winning position we were in halfway through the second half to throw away a 7-point lead, that was the biggest regret I have because I thought we were closer that day.

'Looking back over time, the Dublin team of that era, we always waned late on. Whether it was to do with strength and conditioning, the type of training we were doing, was that a factor in us not closing out games? I think it was. I think we were doing the wrong sort of training, we didn't close out games all that well, in the last five/ten minutes we didn't have enough leaders on the pitch. Physically we struggled, getting tired.

'When it really mattered, we always fell short. But I'll caveat by saying Kerry and Tyrone of that era were two of the greatest teams that ever played the game, and in my opinion they had a better squad of players over time. I just think we came up against such quality. They were simply better than us. More talented footballers, as a team. Mayo weren't, that's why we should have done a number on them that day, and that's the biggest regret. Man for man we were as good. I believe we were good enough.'

Shane Ryan can barely talk about the match: 'Worst defeat ever, I've never been so upset after a game.'

Following the pre-match skirmish, Dublin's Hill-saluting routine attracted far more attention than it had all summer. Some of the players hated it, as did their rivals. Armagh's Justin McNulty says: 'I felt under Pillar Dublin pandered a bit too much to the crowd. I thought it was daft. I think that was probably losing their focus, your focus shouldn't be on the crowd it should be on the task and job at hand. It doesn't matter who's there cheering you on. I think it's part of the reason why they didn't win an All-Ireland. There was too much focus on what was going on off the pitch.'

Mark Vaughan, who came within millimetres of being a hero against Mayo, was equally nonplussed. 'I didn't really buy into it, I wanted to be taking frees instead of doing it before the game, but whatever the manager says goes. I'm only playing under the manager so I just took it and did whatever they said. It probably wouldn't have been my preference, but look, that was what he wanted done.

'Against Mayo I started hitting frees straight after, so I didn't get involved in the messing. That probably would have been my unique strength, I'd never notice anything, I wouldn't even notice I was on the pitch sometimes! I'm unique in that I can just switch on the light at game time. Whether there was 20,000 or 80,000 at the game it wouldn't affect me, I wouldn't even notice, to be honest with you.'

That day ended badly for Vaughan. In a Dublin nightclub, a Mayo man threw a Mayo flag at Vaughan, who threw it on the ground, and got a box in the face – and a broken cheekbone – for his troubles. Jealousy, petty rivalry and – Vaughan's word – 'intolerable' behaviour were just some of the realities those Dublin players endured. Caffrey's 'us against them' mentality was understandable, but in moments like this it probably backfired.

Casey bought into Pillar's methods, but he knows in hindsight the Hill 16 salute looks silly. 'In the moment, you were trying to find every little inch. There was an element of a lot of people would like to see Dublin beaten, so it was to get the fans onside and be one big unit. Would it work now or for any other county? I don't think it would.'

9. The Dirty Dubs

The Blue Book and the Hill 16 salute were at the heart of Dublin's odd mystique under Pillar Caffrey, but there was a more significant psychological change during those years: the Dubs cranked up the verbals.

Saturday, 27 August 2005
DUBLIN v. TYRONE, All-Ireland
quarter-final replay, Croke Park

Ryan McMenamin couldn't resist it. The Dromore man rarely passed on the opportunity to get in an opponent's face. Mossy's missed free was an opportunity.

Tyrone were in the ascendancy, and Dublin needed a score. Quinn missed a kickable free, and McMenamin was straight over to goad his man. When Mossy turned the cheek, he got it in the other ear. The attacker was deflated, and had nowhere to turn.

Quinn and Dublin knew what 'Ricey' was capable of. Earlier in the summer, McMenamin was yellow-carded for dropping his knee on Armagh's John McEntee in the Ulster final replay. He was suspended after the offence was upgraded to a red, but while he missed the qualifier win over Monaghan, his ban was later overturned and he was back for the quarter-final. Dublin were being bullied by a master of the dark arts.

Watching the video analysis afterwards, some tough competitors were furious. Pillar Caffrey, Paul Clarke, Brian Talty and Dave Billings were warriors. They saw Mossy, a cultured footballer, isolated. His teammates were rocked, and nobody had the answer. Something had to be done, and the seeds of change were sown quickly.

Clarke was, of course, an All-Ireland winner and a former All-Star. Obsessed with the hunt for the missing ingredient, he was part of a backroom team leaving nothing to chance in the fight to get Dublin back on the top table. He had been forced to fight before, to come back from the dead. His battles on the pitch were marked towards the end of his playing days by those off it. He was fighting to stay alive.

'We were a very driven group under Pillar, and we did what we had to do,' he said. 'Dublin were getting bullied all over the country, Tyrone were coming in, bullying us, and we felt we had to be stronger. We felt we had to lay down a marker in games. The people involved at that time had very strong principles, and we had to do what we had to do to win matches. Everything we did, our approach to every game, was all building up to coming out of Leinster. We did it so we were ready to tackle the Kerrys or the Corks or Tyrone or Donegal.'

It didn't take much to get through to the players behind closed doors after that Tyrone defeat. The players knew they were being pushed aside by more aggressive opponents when it mattered, and they were ready to go to war for their jersey. This Dublin would no longer be pushed around.

Sunday, 5 February 2006
TYRONE v. DUBLIN, National League
first round, Healy Park, Omagh

A fourth-minute melee, four red cards and nine yellows in front of 12,000 fans and a live TV audience was the ugliest way possible to open the new league season, and it marked out the biggest disciplinary controversy to hit the GAA in years.

Referee Paddy Russell considered abandoning the game, and later admitted he contemplated retiring in the aftermath of his worst experience on a football pitch. The memory of 1995 was still fresh in the minds of Tyrone supporters, who blamed Russell for their defeat in the All-Ireland final to Dublin. First, he'd failed to spot that Charlie Redmond stayed on the field after he had been sent off and, worse again, he disallowed a late Tyrone equalizer because he adjudged Peter Canavan to have touched the ball with his hand on the ground. It proved too much for some of the fans in Omagh, who spat bile at their public enemy number one. Russell, fearful for his safety, looked around for police protection. There was none. Mickey Harte later observed: 'If Paddy Russell had been God Almighty he couldn't have refereed that game today.'

It was a public relations disaster for the GAA. But Pillar Caffrey was ecstatic. The Dublin manager had taken his troops into enemy territory for this televised game, dropped a grenade and marched out with a 3-point win. Special kudos were reserved for the red-carded Alan Brogan and Denis Bastick, and some of the others who got their names in the book – Barry Cahill, Peadar Andrews, Ciaran Whelan and Kevin Bonner. Victory in the Battle of Omagh was as sweet as it came for a team perceived as brittle.

It was a day, the manager's famous Blue Book would go on to boast, when the team 'crossed the line together like a Dublin squad hasn't done in years'.

Paul Casey lived for days like that. 'There was an atmosphere people might say wasn't pretty, but as a sportsman playing in that game, they're the games you want to play in. It was a great battle and it typifies the rivalry between Dublin and Tyrone. While there was respect, when you're in battle you're in battle, and this was huge. It was a great win for us and gave us the confidence to say these northern teams aren't invincible.

'Tyrone, credit to them, they were the benchmark we were setting ourselves against. That game in Omagh probably wasn't pretty for a lot of people watching on, but if you were there you enjoyed the atmosphere, it was tense and it was great for us to come away with a win. That was a satisfying journey home.'

The Central Disciplinary Committee deliberated at length, and five Dublin players were among nine eventually charged on St Valentine's Day with bringing the game into disrepute. But the charges didn't stick, meaning Whelan, Bryan Cullen, Bonner, Andrews and Brogan were clear to fight another day.

Collie Moran, who was captain at the time, was not particularly comfortable with some of what the players were asked to do. But when managers ask you to do something, you do it. 'I would say one of the things after Tyrone in 2005, when the coaches went back through videos after the two games, there certainly was a feeling we were too nice a team and not cynical enough. So there was a deliberate effort to not be so nice. Looking back on it now, I think you'd have to condemn some of it. I don't think it was hugely excessive, or way in excess of what you'd see other teams do, but some of the stuff from some of the players could have been done without.

'For me, to be honest the verbals were something I didn't engage in. But I remember one of the things in my end-of-season reviews with Pillar and the management, they said that I had put a lot of work into my physique and I was naturally a good tackler, putting my body in and breaking ball, which was fine. But they pointed out that over the course of the season I got one yellow card, and insisted that was way too low! The next season I had a rake of yellow cards and I'll admit I certainly engaged in more tactical and cynical fouling, and I got my stats up for yellows.'

25 June 2006
DUBLIN v. LAOIS, Leinster
semi-final, Croke Park

Laois goalkeeper Fergal Byron always relished the opportunity to go head to head with GAA royalty. He fed off the atmosphere generated in Croke Park and got on well with the players he came to know, such as Brogan and Cullen, during a rivalry that spanned close to a decade.

But he came to despise Pillar's team. 'They aren't high in my estimation,' he says, more than a decade later. 'I like Pillar as a person, and don't want to say anything derogatory about him. But something changed in 2006. Anybody that played Dublin in that period, they couldn't stand it. What Dublin were at that stage, the mouthing and all the rest, was so obvious. Everyone just kind of had enough, they were thinking "Come on, Dublin, get back to doing what you do well, get back to playing football and not this bullshit carry-on, because nobody likes it and nobody wants to see it."

'It was just Dublin who behaved that way. You could play

Kerry, even Tyrone and Armagh, they just weren't the same. Dublin weren't like that when we played them in 2003 and in 2005, when they beat us by a couple of points. But in 2006 and '07 it was just rife. The game was over at half-time in '06 yet they continued all the way through.

'In '07, they beat us well, but they were still carrying on the way they were in '06, they were quite mouthy that day in the Leinster final. We got maybe a little bit caught up in the whole thing, we were drawn in. I think Mark Vaughan got a goal, he was in [Darren] Rooney's face and we got dragged into the whole carry-on because we maybe had enough of it at that stage.

'And I'm not even sure he was one of the worst, to be honest, but he was young and impressionable at the time, and maybe it was his character or his nature. Anything he could do to gain a bit of attention, he would. At the end of the day it didn't surprise me he was carrying on the way he was.

'I'm not sure if it was coming from management or where it was coming from. But it was unpleasant. The manner in which they were going about their business was the complete opposite to what you would have expected from players that were playing with them at the time. At the end of the day it's not behaviour that's befitting of professional sports people, or of people acting in a professional environment.'

Dublin had taken a leaf out of the Ricey playbook and developed it some. The players were told to go out and show everyone that Dublin was Dublin. Top dogs, not to be messed with. It didn't matter if they were coming to the end of an extraordinarily close All-Ireland semi-final with Mayo or strolling along at the tail end of a Laois thrashing in Leinster, the job was to hammer it home. We are Dublin.

After the 2007 match, Laois full-back Darren Rooney

accused Dublin of crossing the line. He said, 'Nobody is there to take abuse like that . . . Some of our medical staff got the height of abuse from Dublin players. I was on the ground, getting treated before that, Dublin backroom staff were coming in off the line and one fella came in and jostled me. We'd all know those Dublin lads, but after what happened it will be hard to look at them in the face again.'

Vaughan got in Rooney's face after scoring a goal, making an odd gesture with both hands, and was roundly criticized for his behaviour, But the blond bombshell insists his actions were more innocent than they appeared. It was all inspired by the celebrations seen on the playing fields at the University of Texas in Austin.

'The boys from Crokes were in Texas, fourteen or fifteen of them on the J1,' he laughs a decade later. 'They set it all up. They were ringing me up at night, trying to get me to do a celebration when I scored. We always had a thing every time they were away that I'd do something for them. So I said I'd do the Texas Longhorn in your man's face! That's why I did that to Rooney. It wasn't Pillar at all! The worst thing is my mum worked with Rooney's wife! I only found that out after, of course.'

Shane Ryan is adamant there was no order from on high to mouth off, and he is furious at what he came to see as double standards from Laois in particular. He said: 'There was never a directive that said, "Let's go out and piss these lads off." I think it might have evolved maybe as a defence at the start, other lads were doing it to us. I know against Laois there was one or two years where after we beat them there were interviews with Laois players complaining about Dublin's behaviour, and people were going on about Dublin being a disgrace. There was not a word said about Laois's behaviour, but they were just as bad as anything we did. That really annoyed me. Rooney wasn't the only one, and what annoyed me was things like digs and late tackles and stray fists going in from Laois.

'I'm not saying there weren't verbals because there definitely was, but it was given as much as taken from both sides. I thought it intensified the rivalry over a few years. We'd end up meeting lads playing for Leinster in Railway Cup and you'd get on with them grand, sound lads like.

'When it comes to Leinster championship games, things got more intense. Laois were not on a par with Tyrone at it, though. At that time Tyrone were the masters.'

Collie Moran says: 'One of those games against Laois, I remember there was a big hullabaloo some people raised the next day, Alan pointing at the scoreboard. But of course there was no mention of the fact the reason he did it is because they were hitting him off the ball and that kind of stuff.'

Dubs selector Clarke is unapologetic. 'There were plenty of Laois footballers who'd get up under your skin, like Billy Sheehan, who was very outspoken. On the pitch he'd be giving it loads. They had plenty of players able to dish it out both verbally and physically. You had to be seen to be not pushed around.' Clarke saw no reason to ease up when the game was secure. 'So when we trash a team, we should have taken it handy and not trashed them off the pitch? Come on.'

Laois forward Colm Parkinson spoke out about the 2007 match years later, accusing Casey of pinching and jeering him when Dublin scored. Casey laughs it off. 'I think it was par for the course. By all accounts he brings it up quite a lot. He obviously didn't play against some of the northern teams too often in his career because he'd know all about it if he did. It's looking for the inches, trying to unsettle players. If he's still talking about it now it may have worked.'

Ray Cosgrove liked what he saw in Tyrone and Armagh. He respected their togetherness, and saw no problem following their blueprint. He says: 'We learned from the likes of Armagh and Tyrone. I don't say that lightly. If the Tyrone lads said they weren't doing a bit of sledging then, they are lying through their teeth! And yeah, were our defenders told to give a little bit? Yes, they were. If it meant getting an edge on a fella, to distract him or put him off his game, yeah we were looking to do what it took to get over the line, absolutely. It was becoming more pronounced in the game anyway, it definitely wasn't just Dublin.

'You'd certainly be on the receiving end of a lot of nonsense talk from other fellas. We'd give it. I'm not going to say we were all prim and proper and wouldn't overstep the mark. I can remember Alan getting abused by Conor Gormley. Conor would have given Alan a fierce amount over the years. I don't think he or Ricey would be too offended or upset if I singled them out primarily,' he laughs. 'They were two lads who played on the edge and that's why they were so successful and won three All-Irelands. They knew how to get into someone's head.'

Unlike some of the other Dubs of that time, Vaughan was a natural mouthpiece. In his recollection of events, Armagh were the blueprint for nasty. 'I think a lot of the in-your-face stuff came down to that Armagh lads were doing a lot of it,' Vaughan says. 'I remember going up there and getting it in the ear, but it wouldn't bother me. The more [a defender] chats with me and interacts with me, I know I'm getting on top at some stage. Be it the first five or last five, I'll get a purple patch if he keeps chatting. That used to keep me in games – I'd be talking for the whole game, waiting for that minute where I'd do something or react and try to go after them. Against Armagh, I could be marking Enda McNulty. I wouldn't shut up with him, I'd just kept going and going and going the whole game, waiting for that five-minute spell and eventually got it. It would work on anyone, as eventually most players get annoyed with a lad shouting in your ear.

'Pillar would have been close with Kieran McGeeney from Na Fianna and they'd have done a lot of that in particular when you were up there. I think every person is different; I played with lads like Pat Burke and Davo [Mark Davoren, who would later play for Dublin until injury cut his career short], who'd be quiet but I'd be mouthing off the whole time.

'I'd be talking to him but he wouldn't be listening to me but it kept me focused, so that's what I did. It's unique to whatever you like doing. I don't think really that Pillar went to do it too much, but the reason he probably brought that in was more so that we were getting bullied by Armagh.

'He brought it in to give lads a bit of confidence, so as to not be as intimidated when these lads come after you. So that when they're mouthing off to you that you're not on the back foot, that there's a bit of edge about you.'

Vaughan was a poacher, but he could score from distance with either foot and he struck an exquisite dead ball. He was the type of forward any inter-county manager could work with, and some could build around. His party-boy reputation and juvenile antics disguised a sharp footballing brain. He was rarely rattled, and the ice in his veins provided a cushion from pressure other players would find unbearable, but also a window into the souls of his rivals. He knew instinctively when he held the upper hand. And at club level in particular, that was often.

'To be honest with you, I used to do a lot of it in Dublin club championships back then, and I can tell you for a fact you could see lads crumble in front of you.

'You could just see it even with a lot of the Dublin players when I was marking them in the championships and they'd just crumble. The likes of Ger Brennan at St Vincent's would be able to get up, he'd probably do you, give you a dig; I remember him trying to do me a few times but that was part and parcel – you were both trying to win.

'Without doubt, other lads from the panel would crumble.

'I never really had anyone sent off against me, but you would get guys looking to go after you. It's like sticking a red flag out to a bull. Without doubt I was unpopular. I was known for it. The thing is I knew, but for me winning was the be-all and end-all, and that's how I did it. You're playing to win, I don't care what a guy says to me, and that's being honest. So the way I feel, you know if you're gonna mouth off to me, I'll mouth back at you, you won't get the better of me.

'I didn't lose respect for the lads who wilted, I can under-stand why lads wouldn't want to get involved. I personally tried to say [to others], don't get involved, ignore as much as you can.'

Nobody said he had to take his own advice.

10. Fear

Tyrone and Kerry were the horror films Dublin just couldn't watch. They'd psych themselves up by gorging on the B-movies, but when it came to their bogeymen they couldn't get out from behind the couch.

Mark Vaughan had walked on to the Dublin squad a winner. He couldn't but have that mindset, because he had always won. Legend followed him around like a loyal dog, so everyone had heard the stories. There was the Leinster soccer title he won single-handed for his school, Blackrock College. Vaughan won and converted a late spot-kick to take the final to penalties, before assuming goalkeeping duties in the shoot-out. He saved the first three. Then, faced with the prospect of not getting a chance to take his own kick, he let in the fourth. Then he took off the gloves to score the winner. Sure why not?

He was flash, but what wasn't widely understood was that he was a grafter too. While training with Dublin, only Stephen Cluxton put in as many hours on the training field. He might have come across as a bit of a dummy, but there was nobody on that management team who could teach him more about winning than he already knew. So losing came as quite a shock.

'I'd won all my career,' he says. 'Crokes went five years unbeaten when I played, I'd won the schools All-Ireland with Blackrock, so never had any nervousness or fear playing

Gaelic. Then I came into the Dublin squad and that's when I first saw that fear. You'd notice it. I was fairly young, so a lot of it was I did look up to certain players who I would have kept my eye on. You'd get a feed off them, certain guys . . . Ciaran Whelan in particular I would have looked up to. I always felt, no matter how bad a game was going, these guys would always turn it.'

Dublin strolled through the Leinster championships in 2007 and 2008. After Leinster was sorted, the dynamic changed.

'It was fear of certain teams,' Vaughan says. 'Mayo, Tyrone, Kerry. I was a messer and people would tolerate it, but come those games, against those teams, the tolerance levels dropped. Ciaran Whelan always had his own spot in the dressing room, where he could be quiet and concentrate, but he'd snap at me.

'We had Alan Brogan and so on, but for me Whelan was the man. He'd win the ball, like Darren Magee did for Crokes, so he's the one I'd personally look up to. I've a pretty good read of people, I'd notice on big match days you'd see a kind of change in person, see something different.'

Vaughan believed that the players became more self-aware when out of the Leinster bubble. This wasn't Offaly, this wasn't even Wexford. Perhaps we should act differently? Some played the occasion, rather than the game. And Dublin suffered.

It's worth recalling the words of Paul Clarke: 'Everything we did, our approach to every game, was all building up to coming out of Leinster. We did it so we were ready to tackle the Kerrys or the Corks or Tyrone or Donegal, the teams you had to face up to.' When they actually did come up against those teams, they weren't good enough.

26 August 2007
DUBLIN v. KERRY, All-Ireland
semi-final, Croke Park

Another Croke Park capacity crowd turned out to see the Dubs take on Kerry, the defending All-Ireland champions and favourites. It was a bad-tempered affair, with seven bookings in the opening half, the underdogs doing all they could do to put it up to their technically superior rivals. Several Dublin players were getting in their opponents' faces, which didn't bother their manager in the slightest.

Dublin were 6 down with fifteen minutes remaining, and a goal was on the cards when Shane Ryan burst through, only to be rugby tackled to the ground by Kieran Donaghy. The card would have been black, had that sanction existed. Vaughan, Cullen and Brogan chipped away at the Kerry lead, until the champions regained some semblance of control and eventually prevailed by 1-15 to 0-16.

There was no shame in that defeat, and Kerry went on to regain Sam Maguire by beating Cork in the final. The game marked the end of Pillar's three-year contract, but the board liked what they were seeing. They gave him another year. The players were delighted. 2008 would be, in Caffrey's own words, 'shit or bust'.

Vaughan hit 0-5 against Kerry, with 4 points from dead balls. But he missed an early sitter, one that still niggles. He didn't miss sitters, and he wasn't one for nerves. It was a difficult one to explain. Surveying his teammates, he didn't particularly like what he saw.

'I had missed one free all year. The first one I got [against

Kerry], the easiest one I'd had, I missed. There was that nervousness, and it had built up among the players over time.

'The one I really picked up on was the Kerry game. This
was the first time I'd seen them a little bit on edge. Whelan
stood out because of his demeanour, he was a lot more tetchy,
a little more vocal.'

Ray Cosgrove agrees that there was 'a brittleness' about
that Dublin team, though he offers a different explanation.
'Looking back over time, the Dublin team of that era, we
always waned late on. Whether it was to do with strength
and conditioning, the type of training we were doing, was
that a factor in us not closing out games? I think it was. In the
last five or ten minutes we didn't have enough leaders on
the pitch. Physically we struggled, getting tired. When it
really mattered, we always fell short.'

Kerry's victory could be put down to a very good team
defeating an inferior team. But what happens when an inferior team has clawed back a large deficit to trail by just 1 with
five minutes to go? When that inferior team has in recent
seasons racked up huge scores in some games? Do they have
the tools to pull off a shock? Vaughan believes Dublin did
not have the answers because – unlike Kerry – they had yet
to learn the art of winning.

'I think we were rattled, and that was more so a mindset
than anything. When you look back we were just as good,
but they had the class to get it done.

'We hadn't won in so long. I remember with Crokes in '09,
if we were 5 points behind with ten minutes to go, ninety-
nine per cent of the time I'd be confident we'd win it from
there. That could be in a game where we'd only scored 6
points – how do you expect to score another 6 points in the
last few minutes? But you'd think, "We'll get it done, we'll

get a goal from somewhere." You get into a mindset that you're going to win.

'That's what Kerry had then, particularly with the likes of Gooch up front they just knew if they got him two balls in the last few minutes he's going to score one of them, and if he doesn't score he's going to take out two defenders where you'll get a chance. That was the difference between them and us.

'It's an unknown, when you're not sure. Everyone becomes more tense. You're afraid to pull the trigger, and everyone else missing. But when you know you're going to win there's no fear. Playing without fear is how you win games.'

A team playing with fear, Vaughan says, has 'a mental block, taking a fraction longer than you normally would just to make sure it's the right pass or the right shot. You don't have that [extra time] at inter-county level. You have to know what you're going to do with the ball before you get it most times. There's only the exceptional talents who can take the extra few seconds because they're that good they can make their own time.'

Vaughan's way of keeping focused in the dressing room before a match was to smash balls off the walls. But the routine did not go down well with Whelan and Brogan before the Kerry match.

Vaughan explains: 'My messing before the match wouldn't have been as tolerated that day. Usually they'd turn a blind eye, and let me away. But that day in particular, it was different. The likes of Alan would try and avoid me, whereas on other days when you know you were gonna win you'd have a bit of a laugh, you know what I mean?

'I would have sat beside John Leonard, a good few others would mess, but some of them would get the fear that other lads would point them out or whatever, and they'd branch off when you get to the dressing room.'

Pillar was not a man who liked to shuffle the deck. In Dublin's six matches in 2007, he started just eighteen players, down from nineteen the previous season. Following the Leinster opener with Meath, Mark Vaughan came in for the injured Darren Magee, and there he remained. Bernard Brogan – younger brother of Alan – edged out young Diarmuid Connolly after making his debut in the replay, and endured to devastating effect. Jason Sherlock came in at the expense of Mossy Quinn for the Leinster final against Laois, but otherwise the starting XV was untroubled by change. Match programmes could almost have been printed weeks in advance. By this point an astonishing nine players had started every championship game in Caffrey's reign: Stephen Cluxton, Alan Brogan, Conal Keaney, Barry Cahill, Paul Casey, Shane Ryan, Bryan Cullen, Ciaran Whelan and Paul Griffin.

Pillar's refusal to tinker left some on the margins feeling isolated. It took a long time for Bernard Brogan to convince Pillar he was worthy of his trust. Connolly excited management but was too raw to earn a prolonged championship run. Johnny Magee, who played just a few minutes here and there in the 2007 championship, turned down an invitation to return for the following league campaign. In a heated phone call with the manager, Magee namechecked players he felt were hanging around the squad without much distinction yet were still ahead of him in the pecking order. Caffrey told him he was out of line, and was met with an old-school Johnny Magee response.

Cosgrove was a little less effective in 2007 than he had

been previously, but he was there. Pillar always spoke to him. By 2008, though, he was invisible.

'I'd slipped so far down the pecking order – you know when you're getting number 26 you're not in his plans,' he recalls. 'I remember one game, I didn't even bother putting the jersey on. I knew I wasn't going to be anywhere near the three or four subs coming in, I was so far out of the selection process. I came in after the game to the changing room and the jersey is hanging up on the peg.

'Pillar felt I wasn't good enough or wasn't doing a specific job. When you're not part of the plans, you're not being talked to. That's a signal to say "You're not in my plans, you won't be coming in." He says to other fellas, "If there's a change you'll be coming in."'

It was easier for the regulars. The players were close, the bond with management was real. Shane Ryan thinks of that version of Paul Clarke more as a mate than a coach. The players' determination to do it for the manager, to make it all worthwhile, may have been more of a hindrance than a help, blinding them as it did to the need for calm heads in taxing situations.

'The hype was phenomenal,' says Collie Moran. 'Even first-round games, there were 50,000 people at them. It was a really close-knit squad and management. There was such a desperation among us to get over the line. It was a very passionate squad, and that's what it was. Desperation.'

The scent of Sam Maguire lingered in the air on windy training nights in Artane. It didn't take much to go again after 2007, not with Pillar still around. Shane Ryan was the embodiment of a bolder, physically stronger Dublin. They had the look and feel of champions, but without the only medal that counted in the sock drawer. Pillar's last year was

Ryan's best, marked as it was by an All-Star. 'I was fit, I was confident. I felt that as a team we were flying, getting better every year,' he says.

'I was enjoying my football during the four years with Pillar. It was the first time we started adopting a lot of modern techniques (for that period anyway), modern training methods, strength and conditioning. Myself personally and a number of other players would have seen the biggest improvement in their game, and I would have really enjoyed myself then. I enjoyed every year but this was really when I started seeing and believing we can actually go places. Even though we didn't.

'I don't think I could have played midfield earlier. When I was younger I would have always been confident in my speed and fitness, but that was probably youthful bravado, I didn't realize till I got older that I've actually built up a lot more stamina in my late twenties than my early twenties. I don't think I'd have been able to do the same job at all when I was younger. Experience would have helped as well. Paul Clarke was great to have. I loved training with Clarky, I'd nearly be running out the door for training, to be the first there.

'And the camaraderie! During those four years together we would have all socialized together, lived in each other's pockets, gone away for weekends, with Clarkey included. When I think back, he was only the age I am now when he was doing it. Now I am that age it doesn't seem that old! He'd have been not too far away in age and we'd have got on very well. He was not far enough from playing himself, he knew what it was like.'

Team-building, and bonding, was a core component of the Pillar Caffrey business model. Most players were happy to buy into anything that meant letting off steam when the time was right. Vaughan, renowned for letting off steam when the time was wrong, was not one of those. He would incur Caffrey's wrath on more than one occasion for failing to turn up for nights out with the panel, and he reckons the gaffer's misgivings were warranted.

'I got in little bits of trouble here and there, but he was very tolerant of me,' he says. 'I got in trouble once or twice for going out. I wouldn't really have gone out with a lot of the Dublin lads, so when they did a lot of their days out I wouldn't drink that weekend and then I'd go out the following weekend with my mates. I was recognizable so I'd get seen, and he'd pull me in and say, "We're a team, that was a bonding weekend."

'He's right, that was it. It wasn't anything malicious, but my friends were going out and I wanted to go out with them. Pillar was always pretty easy to deal with, he was a JLO so knew how to handle people. There was a mutual respect. He gave out to me but ninety-nine per cent of the time he was in the right so there was not much I could really say to him.'

'I count my blessings for the four years under Pillar,' says Clarke. 'I actually made better friends from that time with Dublin than I did when I was playing. It was hugely disappointing not to win an All-Ireland. The guys involved were seriously competitive, all winners in their own right. When you see the commitment the players were giving at that time, they were a really great bunch. Some of them playing today, even though they won All-Irelands afterwards, they said – and maybe this was the problem – the best fun and enjoyment they had playing football and training was in that era. We say "Jesus, were we too nice? Where did we go wrong?"'

*

16 August 2008
All-Ireland quarter-final, Croke Park
Dublin 1-8, Tyrone 3-14

All Pillar could think about at the final whistle was getting out of there. Croker, Dublin, Ireland. When his wife came down to see him in the tunnel, he asked her to book a trip abroad, leaving as soon as possible. Not so much a holiday as an escape plan. What else can you do when you have left every ounce of blood and sweat on the training pitch and dressing room, only to suffer a defeat like this?

It rained hard that day, the kind of rain that comes down so heavily it hurts. His Dublin tried everything in the playbook, and came up short to a side that was supposedly in some kind of decline. It mattered little that Tyrone would go on to claim a third All-Ireland under Mickey Harte, because Dublin had been humiliated.

The Dubs marked their season-ender with a session in Coppers, naturally. But there was no fun in it this time. The defeat to Kerry the previous season had been an acceptable way to exit the championship, but this was something else entirely. Was it for this annihilation they had won the Battle of Omagh?

The game was lost as much on the sideline as it was on the pitch, Dublin tactically battered by a master. Harte's positional switches had Dublin in a spin. Key man Bryan Cullen found himself playing much of the first half at full back, picking up Brian McGuigan. Paul Griffin marked three different forwards in that time. Sean Cavanagh enjoyed a tour of Croker with Dublin's nominal full back, Ross McConnell, in his wake. Tyrone took control of midfield, and ownership of any breaking ball.

Tyrone led by 5 at half-time – courtesy of 2 goals – and when they started the second half like a train it was game over. Harte enjoyed the luxury of emptying his bench, as chants of 'Easy, easy' reverberated around Croke Park. The Dublin fans could not understand what had just hit them.

Spain would be Pillar's destination of choice. The county board began looking again at a shortlist.

'The favourites tag weighed heavily,' Collie Moran believes. 'A lot of people had us as favourites, and it was a disaster. There we were: monsoon conditions, conceded all those goals and it was a disaster of a day. It was a really sad end for Pillar and Clarky and Talty, and all those lads.'

Pillar had the players. He had Stephen Cluxton, Bryan Cullen, Cahill, the Brogans, Connolly, an emerging Paul Flynn and Ger Brennan. They looked closely at Michael Darragh MacAuley and helped him overcome back problems. Denis Bastick was there, and Eoghan O'Gara was on the fringes. Jonny Cooper, Darren Daly and Michael Fitzsimons were in the juniors, and the development squads were beginning to bear fruit, even if Pillar's final summer was too soon to enjoy it.

'We felt we touched greatness,' says Clarke. 'I knew in St David's when I saw Connolly and Mark Vaughan kicking balls that I'd never seen anyone do anything like it. And I said if that guy [Connolly] keeps doing what he's doing, keeps his head, he would be one of the best footballers ever. And I said that in 2007. It's not incredible to see what he's doing because I knew that guy was incredible.

'Mark Vaughan was nearly as good as Diarmuid Connolly.

He just didn't follow the same path. Vaughny was doing the same things Connolly was doing with footballs, left foot, right foot, sidelines, fisting, drop kicks. They were doing it all back when they were eighteen, nineteen or twenty years of age. Just brilliant. I'm sorry he didn't go on. He was as good as Connolly back then. We had those guys coming into our group, just a couple of years too soon.'

The 2008 Blue Book asked those who held it in their gear bags to use it 'to the fullest in the hope of gaining that extra inch'. It was a familiar refrain, but for the inches to matter the opponents have to be in sight.

Each of the pages was emblazoned with the words 'Dublin, All-Ireland Champions 2008'.

11. Startled Earwigs

The Dubs were always making little strides. The upward curve in fortunes was gradual, and bumpy, but every time they appeared primed for a breakthrough, they went off the rails again. There were dramatic improvements in under-age coaching and player development, and a more focused approach to fund-raising – all of which helped lay the foundations for success. But it took the arrival of a managerial novice in 2008 to finally knit all the elements together.

It was by no means obvious at the time that Pat Gilroy was the missing link. And well into Gilroy's third championship, in the summer of 2011, it was hard to feel confident that anything fundamental had changed. To that point, Gilroy's Dubs were underachievers in the time-honoured fashion, finding novel ways of raising hopes and then dashing them.

A godson of Heffo's and son of 1963 All-Ireland winner Jackie Gilroy, Pat Gilroy was an engineering graduate who had made a meteoric rise in business. FP2, a facility management company he established, had been taken over by energy firm Dalkia, which then gave him the top job. Between 2002 and 2008, Dalkia's turnover grew from €14 million to €120 million, with a workforce of well over 400 in Swords. He also served as president of the Ireland-France Chamber of Commerce, was a member of the Ibec national council and was secretary of the Energy Institute. The non-sporting CV was longer than the fairly decent sporting one.

Well before Gilroy was offered the Dublin job, what he really wanted was to be Director General of the GAA – and he nearly got it, too. In 2007 he made it on to a shortlist of three to replace the outgoing Liam Mulvihill – despite being just thirty-six years of age, and lacking any experience of Gaelic games administration.

Dusting himself down after narrowly missing the Director General job, Gilroy went on the following year to help his St Vincent's club to Leinster and All-Ireland senior success, providing a fulcrum at full forward in a team that included Mossy Quinn, Diarmuid Connolly and Ger Brennan, and managed by Mickey Whelan. The club was sponsored by Dalkia, the deal orchestrated by Gilroy. He had finished up with the Dubs many years before, and made waves only in the relative anonymity of business. He wasn't a spotlight-craving kind of guy, yet here he was. And then, things got so much bigger when Dublin came calling. Dubs chairman Gerry Harrington, secretary John Costello and a handful of others on the selection committee plumped for Gilroy only after seriously contemplating another swoop for Brian Mullins, who wasn't interested.

Standing by his side (if not exactly shoulder to shoulder) on his coaching ticket was Mickey Whelan – the Vinnies coach, by then approaching seventy. The 2007 version of Whelan was even more impressive on paper than the 1996 version. He was an All-Ireland-winning coach, albeit at club level, and had earned a sport science doctorate from DCU. It was Heffo, of course, who had talked him into taking the Vincent's job, just as he had the Dubs job in 1996; and again in 2008 it was Heffo who urged him to join Gilroy's team. Some saw it as a shot at redemption. Whelan just felt it was a job he had to do.

Gilroy would need a decent start as Dublin manager to shift the focus away from his own inexperience. He was well connected – a god in Vinnies, with a direct line to Heffo – and it may have been felt that he'd jumped the queue. He decided before he even got the gig that he wouldn't obsess over the PR side of the job, as Lyons had done. He treated the media as he did any adversary – with respect, but with plenty of distance. Gilroy didn't feel the need to fill any more pages than were absolutely necessary. Whereas Lyons had sought to use the hype to his advantage, Gilroy did whatever he could to dampen expectations.

Within the camp, expectations were modest enough. 'The guru, me bollix,' laughs clubmate Eamon Heery. 'I had Pat Gilroy at under-15, myself and Ski Wade. He was that fucking bad we put him in goals to stop the ball going over the bar!'

Gilroy was a disciplinarian, as some of his players and soon-to-be-former players would find out. He was also a master of disguising his thoughts. When the occasion called for it, though, he could be ruthlessly forthright. Players were ordered to fall in, or shuffle off.

He kept his inner circle tight. In addition to Mickey Whelan, Paddy O'Donoghue was one of his selectors, a colleague from Trinity College days. He identified key people to carry out the important tasks, and set them loose. When he trusted a person to do a job, he didn't need to micro-manage. For starters, there weren't enough hours in the day.

When Gilroy was unveiled, the players wondered: 'Has he actually ever managed before?' But upon their introduction, they were floored. Collie Moran recalls: 'He wasn't even an outsider, because he wasn't even seen as a contender. There was even talk about Dublin possibly going outside the county in their search for a manager for the first time.

'When it was announced that Pat was taking charge, it was a massive surprise. Nobody really knew much about him and he wasn't coming in with much experience. But I remember well that first night the squad met him in Parnell Park. There was no razzmatazz or anything about his presentation or what he said – but straight away, it was very clear that he was a straight talker. You could tell immediately he was a serious operator, that he had a huge passion for Dublin GAA, and there was a sense among the players leaving the meeting that, yeah, he was the right man for the job.'

One of Gilroy's first acts as manager was to send twenty-one-year-old Diarmuid Connolly home from a training camp in La Manga in January 2009. The pair knew each other inside out from the club, and Gilroy's reaction to a breach of discipline laid down a marker for the rest of the squad. The fallout didn't prove terminal, and Dermo was included in Gilroy's first league squad, but it sent out a message that the days of Pillar and his tolerance for messing were gone.

Dublin were only three weeks into their preparations when they took on Tyrone – again – under the Croke Park lights in the first round of the league. It marked the beginning of the GAA's 125th-Anniversary celebrations, which whipped the hype up beyond more than a 31 January fixture normally would. Gilroy, who couldn't have asked for a more awkwardly high-profile beginning to a tenure that he wished to keep as low-profile as possible, was edgy in his media duties that week. Dublin were decent in a 1-18 to 1-16 defeat, running the All-Ireland champions closer than many expected. Denis Bastick was recalled to solve the problematic full-back position, David Henry relocated to the attack complete with armband, and the evergreen Jason Sherlock – Gilroy's pal from '95 – was at full forward. Massacre avoided, the manager publicly relaxed. Privately, there would be no letting up.

Conal Keaney took the captaincy for the second game, against Galway, and declared he would be hopeful to keep the job long term. His new manager would eventually prove to have other ideas entirely.

Dublin were blitzed by Galway in Salthill, going down by 3-12 to 0-13. A 0-13 to 1-8 win over Donegal in Ballyshannon was followed up by a dire 0-20 to 1-12 defeat to Derry in Parnell Park. Following draws with Mayo and Kerry, the Dubs finished up their Division 1 odyssey with a 5-22 to 0-10 win over already-relegated Westmeath. Dublin finished 1 point outside the drop zone, but by the end of the campaign they had Connolly back in good scoring form, Darren Magee impressive in midfield and Kilmacud Crokes All-Ireland club winner Mark Davoren appearing a serious option at full forward. Alan Brogan had returned, Ger Brennan was proving immovable at centre back and they were beginning to look in patches a serious team. Dublin were physical, hard running and athletic. The platform was set.

Summer rolled around fast, and Mickey Whelan was excited by what he saw. He believed this Dublin side were the most physically primed he had ever seen and was convinced they would have the edge on any opponent thrown their way. The players rowed in completely behind their new overlords, impressed to a man by what they were seeing. Whereas under Caffrey the number of players called upon in the white heat of championship action was strictly limited, Gilroy found a way to keep everyone motivated. Paul Casey, no longer a regular starter, said: 'Pat was a very shrewd, clever man. He was the brains behind the operation. Mickey Whelan, as his trainer, was top class.

'It was all ball work, running with the ball. Mickey was always a step ahead of his time. He's the godfather of GAA coaching as far as I can see. It was a big thing for Dublin, to have a club team that won an all-Ireland. When you have four or five fellas in the squad who have been through that, it brings confidence to the team.

'Pat would have you guessing a lot of the time – where you are and what your role is. Then you might have a conversation and he'd give you the confidence that said, 'OK, I have a role here and this is what I can aim for.' Whether in the back of his mind he really thought you might have a role in a Leinster final only he knows, but he gave players the confidence, that goal to aim for. It meant the intensity of training and matches was so much higher.'

Dublin struggled to a 0-14 to 0-12 win over Meath in the Leinster opener, hitting 17 wides and just 3 points in a woeful second half on 9 June. Three players made their championship debuts, while Shane Ryan and Ciaran Whelan were dropped to the bench. Keaney and Alan Brogan did most of the damage in front of more than 75,000 people. Old warhorses Whelan and Sherlock were sprung from the bench towards the end, but did little to stem the unease that was seeping through Dublin's play. An injury to Davoren proved season-ending, the full forward tearing his cruciate.

Connolly and Sherlock were back in the starting XV for the Leinster semi-final against Westmeath three weeks later, with Rory O'Carroll making his bow in defence. It was a game that really marked Bernard Brogan out as a star for the Hill 16 faithful, Alan's younger brother registering 2-8 in a 4-26 to 0-11 annihilation. Almost 51,500 fans watched Sherlock dictate the play from the off in a game devoid of any obvious intensity.

The Dubs were back in Croker a fortnight later to see off Kildare and add a fifth Leinster title in a row. As a game it was everything the semi-final wasn't, a thriller in front of 74,453, in which 33 out of 35 scores came from play. Dublin stormed out of the blocks and threatened to blow the Lilies away, but Ger Brennan was sent off after eighteen minutes and the Dubs found themselves 0-12 to 2-5 down at the break. The younger Brogan operated from the 40 in the second half and was Dublin's matchwinner, lashing over 7 points, including some key late scores in a 2-15 to 0-18 win.

And that's where Dublin's highlights reel for 2009 ended. They booked their place in the All-Ireland quarter-final with Kerry, who had been in dreadful form. Gilroy's men went in as favourites, but left humiliated. A year on from the capitulation under Caffrey, a new man had presided over another horror show. They were, in Gilroy's own words, akin to 'startled earwigs', beset by nerves, rudderless on the big stage against a team of Colm Cooper, Tadhg Kennelly, Declan O'Sullivan, Tomás Ó Sé, Marc Ó Sé and Paul Galvin. They were beaten, according to Gilroy, to everything, everywhere. In the first half, fourteen balls were drilled into Dublin's full forward line, of which three bore fruit.

1-24 to 1-7 makes for grim reading. When 81,890 are there to see it, there are no holes big enough to swallow you up.

The build-up had been good. The plans were in place. Kerry had been annihilated in Munster by Cork and they struggled past Longford, Sligo and Antrim in the qualifiers. Still, by all accounts, the Dubs did not underestimate their opponents. But they didn't have the tools to withstand the Kingdom's power, and they froze like rabbits in the spotlight.

Or, more accurately, they ran around in a panic like insects from under a rock.

Within an hour of the game ending, Gilroy was obsessing about the following year. Even as the team gathered in the Gibson Hotel, he spoke about improvements. He had hoped that he could take Pillar's squad, make a few minor adjustments, extract the final five per cent needed, and win an All-Ireland. That hadn't happened, but he knew what had gone wrong and he was itching to get working again. Gilroy knew that if Dublin were to shed the nearly-men tag, he would have to break down everything that had gone before, and build it back up from scratch. It meant a tactical overhaul, and also a change in personnel.

Mark Vaughan, who made a late appearance as sub in the Westmeath league game, had already become the first major casualty of Gilroy's professional regime. The pair failed to hit it off from the outset, the animosity there for anyone to see. Vaughan, who struggled consistently with back problems, asked Gilroy for a break early in 2009. They agreed on a six-week leave of absence. Vaughan was only back doing drills ahead of the Kerry game when he was spotted in Café en Seine, and that spelled the end of his inter-county career at the age of twenty-three.

'If I played two games in quick succession I would be crippled for weeks afterwards,' says Vaughan of his troublesome back. 'The travel time in the car is the worst thing possible for it. So I came back and asked could I have a six-week break. I needed a break as I was playing for two years straight. Then the argument happened. I was probably too stubborn to apologize, although I'm not sure he'd have taken me back.'

Vaughan never really loved the Dubs anyway, not like he loved Kilmacud Crokes. The Dublin players weren't his friends. His pals were at the club, people he would run through walls for. Playing for Dublin was an honour, sure, but not the realization of a dream. He may not have been professional enough, in hindsight, to warrant a long career in blue. Perhaps if he had loved it a bit more he might have tried to negotiate with Gilroy, but what's the point in fighting for something you could take or leave?

'For whatever reason, I get a way bigger drive out of playing with lads I hung around with,' he says. 'It's probably embarrassing if you've had a bad game, because you've let those lads down that you hang around on a daily basis. It would give me an additional drive, but I never had that with Dublin. I wasn't really hanging around with those guys as such, it was more a job. Don't get me wrong – you enjoy it, but you're going out with a purpose, whereas I'd do my best stuff when I'd go out with enjoyment and have a laugh in training.'

Still just in his early thirties, Vaughan remains a Crokes stalwart – and hasn't changed his approach to the game. 'I don't really warm up, but I'd go out with a ball for forty minutes. I'm pretty much the last one going out, of our age group, still playing. I'm probably the only guy who never warmed up, or stretched at all. I'd stretch a hammer, that's it, it's the way I was. A lot of lads are different, and I think it would have been one of my downfalls because I wouldn't have taken it as seriously as a lot of other guys. I'd pretty much given up three summers with Dublin, missing J1s. The first two I knew I wasn't going to start and some lads quit to go on the J1, but I stuck it out. To be honest with you I wouldn't have minded going on the J1. You can't really regret playing for Dublin, you're probably never gonna get the opportunity again if you do go away, but I think every lad would like to go on a J1.'

Allowances were always made for Alan Brogan, who would often come back to pre-season training much later than the other players. It caused some minor unrest, but his various injury niggles and his status as a blue-chip player provided him with leverage other players didn't enjoy. Vaughan had no problem with that. 'He was a unique talent, so that was one of the things I never really minded. There was animosity, but I had no problem. If he's a better player than me then he's a better player than me. I never understand other lads getting annoyed about those things.'

Vaughan felt that the travel required for a player with full-time work commitments was a huge ask, but he knew that Gilroy was a man who didn't make or listen to excuses.

The Dublin footballers were used to worrying about the likes of Kerry, Mayo and Tyrone. Now they faced a threat from an unexpected quarter. By 2009 the Dublin hurlers, for so long the footballers' under-achieving siblings, were making strides – and some of the footballers started thinking about switching codes. David Henry, Conal Keaney, Connolly, Shane Ryan and Dotsy O'Callaghan were some of the senior footballers who always felt their imaginations drawn to the small ball.

The hurlers won the 2006 Division 2 league title under Tommy Naughton, and the arrival of Clare All-Ireland winner Anthony Daly as boss for the '09 season marked them out as an outfit with serious ambition. O'Callaghan forged an excellent career with the hurlers, and by 2009 Ryan saw fit to join him. He was no longer one of Dublin's marque players, swapping 2008's All-Star year for a season on the margins under Gilroy. His seven-minute cameo in the Kerry game showed up the thirty-year-old his new place in the pecking order.

Daly came knocking, which gave Ryan something to think about. Hurling was his first love. He felt the footballers were going somewhere – but weren't they always just going somewhere? Would they ever actually get there? Ultimately, Gilroy gave him all the reason to leave he needed. The pair sat down for a ten-minute chat, which turned into something much longer. Gilroy's end-of-season chats became infamous, the death knell for a number of inter-county careers. He wasn't always spot on in his judgement: Jonny Cooper, for one, would later be told he wasn't good enough.

'I made the decision to walk,' says Ryan. 'It was actually something I'd thought about, and a few of us used to chat about how wouldn't it be great to go back to the hurlers for a couple of years? I don't know if we were ever serious, but when the solid offer came, I had to think. The year hadn't gone so well with me under Pat. I was very up-front about it. It was all above board, we were very cordial with each other, and there's no bad feelings really. Every player had a meeting with Gilroy, some very honest words were spoken. I had a number of grumbles, we spoke about them, talked it out, the meetings were supposed to be ten minutes each but mine went on for forty-five minutes.

'I got a lot off my chest and he told me his side of it, we never got angry or abusive, it was a good honest chat, but ultimately it boiled down to "I've an opportunity to do something with a different team, and I don't know if I'll be able to do what I want to do with the footballers." Not that he ever said it, but I don't think I was the type of player he wanted, he wanted a different type of player. I can't speak for [Ciaran] Whelan, but I think he found that, too. I would have stuck around if the hurling offer didn't come, because I wasn't ready to stop playing inter-county.

'I thought, "If I don't do it now I never will. I might regret it." When I was a teenager I was more of a hurler. I came late to football, and never played minor for Dublin. I never did football until second year U-21 and I had already done a couple of years hurling at that stage. So it was kinda like going back to where I started, to see if I can still do it.

'I thought about it long and hard, had lots of chats with my dad, who was very good. I thought I could go back and give it a lash with the footballers, but I didn't think I'd get anywhere. As it turned out, Pat was the right man for the job. Maybe he was right to do it and maybe he did need new lads in there. Who knows, maybe I could have stayed and maybe I could have fought hard and gotten more of a run, but we'll never know.'

Keaney would eventually join Ryan for Daly's hurling revolution. Gilroy was extremely unimpressed with the Ballyboden man's contribution against Kerry in 2009, and despite his scoring feats for the Dubs he would pay the price for it in 2010 after a poor showing against Meath. He always kept his hand in with the small-ball game, something Gilroy wasn't too keen on either. Ironically enough, while Gilroy ended the post-match drinking culture in the Sunnybank, the hurlers would find themselves back in the Glasnevin haunt under Daly, who had been introduced to Peter Garvey by former Clare selector Harry Bohan.

Ciaran Whelan had that chat with his manager too, and the result was just as inevitable. After a storied inter-county career, he would finish up without that All-Ireland winner's medal, his last contribution as a substitute being in the quarter-final annihilation by Kerry. On the face of it, Dublin were not that much further along than they were in 1996 when he started. Sure, they were winning Leinsters, and could sometimes score at will, but despite everything that had gone into it, the big days exposed the vital missing ingredients.

The star midfielder for fourteen seasons must have felt as though he had walked under every ladder on the way up. At a few sunsets shy of thirty-two, he wasn't the swashbuckling player of old, and he struggled with recovery. He could still have played a part, but Gilroy wasn't sold on a player who was becoming increasingly belligerent as he got older. In a 2008 league game against Meath, he drew condemnation for his part in a game that saw five reds and eleven yellow cards. Whelan, by now an elder statesman who should have known better, was sent off for punching Seamus Kenny. The referee, Paddy Russell, probably felt he had seen all this somewhere before. People close to Whelan believe he saw 2008 as his best chance of glory, and he struggled badly to shake off the despondency after that Tyrone defeat.

Gilroy preferred to concentrate on new blood rather than squeezing the last few drops out of the old. Whelan's introduction after fifteen minutes against Kerry would once have triggered a Dublin revival, or at least an aggressive resistance. But his impact was negligible, and his retirement predictable. He might have stayed on for a last hurrah if he was adequately cajoled. He wasn't.

'I'm disappointed for Ciaran Whelan, a phenomenal footballer with whom I had a very good relationship, that he didn't win an All-Ireland,' says Tommy Lyons. 'He battled awful hard. He was very unlucky to come in in '96 and leave when he did. But as I keep saying to people, Ciaran Whelan carried a jersey for Dublin, when he gave it to Michael Darragh MacAuley he gave him a good jersey, and to Brian Fenton now. To me, he is one of a lot of really good footballers who didn't win an All-Ireland, but there are a lot of good footballers in other counties that never get a sniff of an All-Ireland.'

Paul Casey was one veteran who decided to hang on. He watched as one by one the old warhorses departed the scene, but he felt he had enough in the tank to keep going. 'Conal and Shane probably wanted to give the hurling a go. They probably saw themselves that they could be regulars [in the hurling team] and their position in the football might be in doubt. With Ciaran, it was a question, could he keep going? He'd given so much service to the jersey – could he go again?

'Look, it was probably bad timing for them in hindsight. Could they have offered something to the squad? Definitely. Would it have changed the course of success? It definitely wouldn't have diminished it anyway, and they would have had huge roles to play. But ultimately it came down to the players' calls and whether they were willing to give that extra commitment after giving so much.'

With Gilroy opting for morning and evening sessions for the 2010 season, that commitment was only going to become more intense. The manager wanted much, much more.

12. Money, Money, Money

It's impossible to talk about Dublin in the chaotic years between 1995 and 2011 without talking about something that GAA people have sometimes preferred to pretend doesn't exist: money. The hiring of Pat Gilroy coincided almost exactly with the global crash that began in 2008 – a crash that hit Ireland especially hard.

The Dubs were effective fundraisers in the boom years. They were also great at putting bums on seats, filling Croke Park for Leinster turkey shoots. The Merry Ploughboy pub in Rathfarnham, formerly owned by 1970s Dubs icon Sean Doherty, was steeped in GAA. In 2006, new owners Liam and Eoghan Heneghan took over and in time began arranging buses to take its fanatical customers to Croker for championship games. But where once they packed two buses for the short trip north, by 2011 they struggled to fill one. 'People couldn't spend the money on a ticket for themselves and the family, the numbers fell way down,' says Eoghan Heneghan. 'They were still there,' Liam explains. 'But there was a difference between going yourself and with the kids. Or having a few drinks and not having any. When the economy hit, you couldn't but notice. I remember that great GAA pub, Hill 16, being very grateful for our bus stopping by. Times were tough.'

In the Sunnybank Hotel, regulars would skip a month of ordinary Saturday night pints in order to save for the Dublin days, which remained the highlights of many people's lives.

The crowds kept piling into Croke Park, but wallets were emptier, sacrifices taken to get there far greater.

In a time of suffering, the Dubs should never have been immune. Yet somehow, they were.

Dublin GAA was always better funded than other counties. When brands appeared on county jerseys for the first time in 1991, Dublin were ahead of the pack. Former Dubs star Bill Kelly, an Executive Director of department store Arnotts, agreed a two-year £50,000 deal with the county board. In comparison, Sean Boylan's Meath made do with £30,000 over the same period from meat suppliers Kepak.

The partnership lasted for eighteen years, Seamus Deignan picking up where Kelly left off, with the Henry Street retailer acting as a de facto Dublin superstore – and a tailor to the players on big All-Ireland days. In 2002, the company even stepped in to help fund Dublin's end-of-year holiday to South Africa when the Leinster Council declined the opportunity to do so – despite the boost made to its coffers by the county's provincial championship run. By 2009, Arnotts were paying around €600,000 a year to the Dubs, partly from the proceeds of merchandise sales.

Yet Gilroy wasn't impressed with the financial situation he inherited. In 2010, Dublin were third, behind Tipperary and Cork, on the amount spent on the county teams, shelling out €1.2 million, with rivals Kerry spending €1.1 million.

Gilroy felt Dublin were woefully underfunded if they were to effectively challenge for an All-Ireland, and he set about overhauling the commercial structure. He asked the county board to hire a full-time commercial manager. When he was told they didn't yet have the funds to do so, Gilroy decided to do the job himself.

Vodafone won the contract to sponsor the Dubs from 2010, Gilroy's second season as boss, on an initial three-year deal at €800,000 per year, with the option for a further three if both parties were satisfied with how the arrangement was going. Dublin were in demand, and they opted for Vodafone over another communications behemoth, Meteor, which was also in the running. (There was also interest from the banking sector, despite its own obvious difficulties.) Already sponsors of the GAA All-Stars and the football championship (and long-time sponsors of Manchester United and the McLaren Formula 1 team), Vodafone saw an opportunity in Gaelic games' most famous underperformers. With Vodafone on board, the Dubs were out on their own financially. By comparison, Cork's sponsors at that time, O2, paid about €200,000 per year. The Dublin county board spent in excess of €1.7 million in 2011, while the vast majority of other counties were forced to rein in their expenditure in light of the economic collapse. Kerry's outgoings were reduced to less than €800,000. Dublin splashed out more than Fermanagh, Louth, Longford, Sligo, Derry and Monaghan combined.

The Vodafone deal was worth a lot more than the Arnotts one, but Dublin would have to work harder for the money. Player appearances were extremely rare during the Arnotts years, meaning stars from Keith Barr's day all the way up to Ciaran Whelan were unlikely to be seen in the newspapers holding models on their arms in front of the season's brightest fashion range. Vodafone, which had run ad campaigns in the recent past for David Beckham, not unreasonably wanted their brand stamped in the psyche of the average Dublin fan, and not just on the jersey.

Vodafone were initially bemused at Dublin's lack of commercial management. The player-appearances culture was only slowly being introduced, and on more than one occasion players failed to show up for appointments. The game may have been amateur in ethos, but the big brands shelling out millions of euros demanded professionalism. Dublin were competing not just with the other major counties but also with other sports, Leinster rugby (who won their first of three European cups in 2009) being the most obvious case in point.

To address this, Gilroy launched Project Blue, a commercial vision for Dublin. He hired a full-time fundraiser for the county board, and wooed a new wave of secondary commercial partners. He envisaged a new website dedicated to flogging merchandise, and even a mascot – Bud the Dub – but neither materialized. He was forced to shelve the website under the sponsorship deal, as Vodafone had paid to rebuild the official site and were unhappy with the idea of a competing site. County board officials – including the influential country secretary – were curious to see where having a coach-cum-general manager would lead them.

Bertie Ahern knew Gilroy's dad, and was in Croke Park when Jackie crossed for Eamon Breslin to head the ball in the net against Laois in 1964. Now, he was bowled over by the novice manager, immediately recognizing him as a cut above the rest, and willing to help in any way he could. 'We were just trying to get contacts,' he says. 'Pat wanted more doctors, more physios, and that required a few quid. They had Arnotts, but they needed more to fund what Pat was trying to do. The money wasn't there, so he had to do it himself.

'If Pat didn't do that, he wouldn't have built the team of 2011. In fairness to Pat it was all done very formally and correctly with John Costello, but we were out just trying to get people to help. Then of course we got the big deal [with Vodafone]. Pat built up a very professional thing but it didn't happen overnight. He took it to a new level. He came in with a plan.'

Commercial sponsorship would be the main revenue-generator for Dublin, but they also had the Parnell Park pass scheme – limited season tickets for supporters – which continued to provide a significant six-figure sum per annum. Gilroy also wanted wealthier Dublin patrons to dig a little deeper into their pockets and help put the Dubs back on the map. Friends of Dublin football were fundraising around the clock. Past players were often called on to use their connections, and Tommy Lyons was always happy to lend a supporting hand.

Dublin had been moving from training ground to training ground for years without ever having a full-time home. Gilroy was done roaming, and under his management the Dubs moved to a DCU training facility at St Clare's in Glasnevin. It consisted simply of a pitch and a pre-existing building – dubbed 'the Bunker' – which he had renovated to suit the team's needs. Attached to a nursing home and tucked away up a small avenue, the set-up was a symbol of Gilroy's Dublin – low-key, functional, and effective. The pitch itself was overlooked by homes, but the off-field work was done away from prying eyes against a backdrop of bare concrete-block walls. On arrival, the players walked into a classroom, where they would pore over video analysis. An attached kitchenette was basic. That fed through to a warren of changing and training rooms, decked out with equipment for monitoring fluid loss and recovery – common now but not in 2009. Drawing on an extensive list of business contacts who were happy to help with alterations and facilities for less than the going rate, Gilroy secured a decent deal for his employers.

With a revolutionized commercial structure in place, targeted fundraising and modern training facilities to go along
with its large playing population, Dublin had the potential to
be unrivalled. Once they overcame the inevitable teething
problems associated with change, they were primed to match
off-pitch ambitions with success on it.

13. 'See you all in Coppers'

To the untrained eye, Bernard Brogan – Hill 16 darling and scorer-in-chief – was the ultimate forward. But to his manager, he was someone who wasn't working hard enough for the team. Defending from the front was an art Brogan had never been asked to master – or even pay too much heed to – during a career in which being the best came naturally to him. Pat Gilroy wasn't content to let Brogan loose on defences if he didn't play his part in keeping scores out at the other end.

Gilroy, one former player says, 'fucked with Brogan's head'. The former player recalls: 'Bernard was used to being the best, simple as. But Pat wouldn't tolerate a forward not putting in a shift, no matter who he was, and let him know all about it. He'd tear into him in training. Gilroy wanted him to operate as part of a collective, not as an individual.' Brogan was a self-confessed 'selfish full forward' who would 'not track back'. That changed in 2010, when the forwards were invited to buy in to the defend-from-the-front mantra, or take a hike. It took a while, and a spell on the sidelines in the early part of the 2010 league campaign, but Brogan did eventually row in. By the end of 2010 he would be footballer of the year.

Brogan's transformation was only one facet of Gilroy's revamp. The manager hated the sledging culture that had taken hold in Caffrey's teams, and he banned it. He demanded that his team respect their opponents, no matter who they

happened to be. He also hated the razzmatazz that Pillar or
Lyons had fed off. There would be no Ray Cosgrove-style
goal celebrations, no saluting the Hill. Gilroy preferred not
to rely on the barnstorming individual genius of, say, a Ciaran
Whelan, who would occasionally maraud down the sideline
and sling one over from forty-five yards. Such moments were
exciting, but the style of play that produced them was not, to
his mind, effective. He introduced punishing 6 a.m. sessions
at the Bull Wall. It was a lot to ask of any player with commitment issues.

Gilroy spent hours in video analysis of his side's games.
He identified players who wouldn't track back, or who gave
up too easily in certain situations, and he took action. Mike
McCarthy's part in Colm Cooper's goal early in the 2009
quarter-final was a particular annoyance; the Kerry centre
half back was allowed to saunter through the Dublin defence
unchecked before providing the final pass. One player says
that Gilroy 'went through that squad with a knife and said,
"Gone, gone, gone, gone." They kept lads they felt were
made of the right stuff and built on it.' By the end of the 2010
Championship, veterans Whelan, Ryan and Sherlock were
gone, the once-pivotal Keaney reduced to a substitute role.
Not everyone who finished up did so gladly. 'Some of the
lads were very bitter over it,' a former player says.

Mickey Whelan identified a number of players who he felt
could offer Dublin another dimension. Eoghan O'Gara, a
rangy junior star of 2008 with a questionable technique, was
one; Michael Darragh MacAuley, an extremely unorthodox
basketball player who had been on Caffrey's radar but who
had endured fitness struggles, was another. Early on, the
management team drilled into its players that hard work
wasn't optional. Players who didn't reach the requisite

standards were sent home from training and told not to bother coming back the following night unless they were willing to do what their colleagues were willing to do.

Dublin teams of the previous five years had all shared one recognizable trait: an inability to see out tight games. When the football was flowing, they were unstoppable, but when backs were to the wall, they were consistently found wanting. Mickey Whelan's drills reflected a determination to alter that tendency. There were small-sided games in tight spaces, which meant more hits for players on the ball and with less time to think. The idea was to find some way of modelling the white heat of August and September championship action. Players had real-game situations drilled into them every morning and night, by a man who had suffered hurt as Dublin manager in the 1990s but who was now in his element: a coach doing what he did best.

The 2010 league campaign kicked off with a win against Kerry in Killarney, Paul Flynn and Eamon Fennell shining in the Dubs' first away win against the Kingdom since 1982. MacAuley was effective on the 40 in a side that contained just five of the team humiliated the previous summer. James McCarthy – son of John – was introduced to the starting XV, and endured a torrid time at the hands of Paul Galvin. Gilroy let his debutant see out the seventy minutes. McCarthy, who would have welcomed the shepherd's crook, later told how it was the making of him, and a mark of the manager's faith in his abilities. Kevin McManamon took his chance to shine with 2 points, while sub Bernard Brogan – on the trajectory of a steep learning curve – came on to score a point. The new-look Dublin also showcased Cian O'Sullivan and Philly McMahon.

Infectious hard work was a recurring theme in the league

as the Dubs overcame Derry and then Mayo, Brogan goaling after once more being introduced to secure a 1-point win in Castlebar. The St Oliver Plunkett's man was in from the start against Monaghan and hit 1-6 in a 5-point home win. Defeats to Cork and Galway followed, Brogan registering 11 points against the Tribesmen before Dublin finished off by routing Tyrone in Omagh by 2-14 to 1-11. Brogan hit 6 points from play and 8 in total, condemning their old rivals to the drop.

Paul Casey, survivor of the '06 battle of Omagh, says: 'There wasn't the same hype, but we went up and beat them. David Hickey [a selector at the time] often makes the point that it was a huge game in Pat's tenure. When someone like David says that, you definitely pay attention.'

Everything was in place for a serious assault on the 2010 championship – and then it all fell apart. Dublin failed to show up for the Leinster quarter-final against Wexford, trailing 0-8 to 0-2 at half-time. Bernard Brogan ultimately proved the match winner with 2-4 in a game the Dubs won only after extra time, although he did boot seven wides. Both Denis Bastick and Ger Brennan saw red in normal time, with the impressive sub O'Gara lucky to avoid a second yellow.

Far from a one-off dip in form, the Wexford performance was a warning – or should have been. The Dubs' 11-point defeat to Meath in the provincial semi was the biggest margin between the two sides in almost half a century. Meath's extraordinary 5-9 to 0-13 goal blitz left Dublin at the mercy of the qualifiers for the first time since 2004.

Alan Brogan later defined it as a watershed in Dublin's development under Gilroy. Dublin felt they were very close to a real Championship tilt, and turned up expecting to beat their old rivals. Instead, a young defence shipped a glut of goals – and the inquest began immediately afterwards. Each player was forced to watch match footage which showed up the moments when they failed to track back, or work hard for the team. It made for grim viewing.

Gilroy singled out Brogan, Mossy Quinn, Keaney, Barry Cahill and Bryan Cullen for particular criticism. Those experienced players, he felt, left their rookie defence exposed. Only Brogan was spared the chop. Keaney left the panel later that year.

Gilroy would continue to insist that his forwards track back – but he was also forced to reconsider a defensive system that could disintegrate so completely. He insisted thereafter that Dublin always have six men at the back. That meant full backs and half backs staying put. Brogan said: 'It took a crisis to make us realize we were like any other team if we didn't work for one another. It was Meath who had shown us the folly of our old ways.'

The qualifiers are usually about hitting the road in search of redemption, but Dublin stayed right where they were. Croker was again the venue for all three of their back-door games, won with relative ease against first Tipperary, then Armagh and finally Louth, setting up a quarter-final showdown with Ulster champions Tyrone. On 31 July, Dublin set about dismantling their most illustrious rivals in a performance right out of Mickey Harte's own play book. It was in that game in front of 62,749 that the 6 a.m. sessions in an unforgiving Bull Wall finally paid dividends. A ravenous Dublin devoured their rivals, eating up every inch of territory on their way to what was their most impressive win in many years.

Bernard Brogan kicked 9 points, and O'Gara cemented

his status as a cult hero with a goal, but the victory was built at midfield: MacAuley and Ross McConnell were unplayable. Stephen Cluxton, outstanding in goal, earned one of the biggest cheers of the day when he slotted over a 45. Nothing to it.

The supporters dared to dream again. Liam Heneghan, for one, kept thinking about Sam Maguire. He was emptying the keg room of The Merry Ploughboy when the lyrics of a song began forming in his head. 'There hadn't been a song written about the Dubs, really, since Derek Warfield wrote about Jimmy Keaveney being sent off against Offaly in 1979,' he says. 'The momentum was building again, we'd navigated the qualifiers. I thought it was time for something new.'

Heneghan sat down and wrote a song, recorded it – and ahead of the All-Ireland semi-final against Cork, he had a YouTube sensation on his hands.

'Sam is coming home, back to Molly Malone.
He's tired of cutting cabbages in Kerry and Tyrone.
He misses Anna Liffey, the coddle and the crack.
Sam is coming home, he wants a welcome back.'

Sam, it turned out, was not coming home. Cork had no business winning a game Dublin dominated for large spells, but they were a team accustomed to playing on that stage and in their sixth successive semi-final appearance they made that experience count. Dublin's blue wall resisted the best of what the Leesiders threw at them – until concentration levels began to wane. McConnell conceded a converted penalty in the fifty-third minute, and a late blitz for the Rebels saw them edge into the lead for the first time in the sixty-ninth minute. Brogan's 1-7 was enough to mark him out as the season's outstanding footballer, but it was Cork who would win what mattered the most. Having beaten the better team, they went on to pip surprise package Down in the final.

Dublin and Cork would lock horns again the following April in the league decider, following a near-flawless campaign for Gilroy's men in which they scored 16 goals. Casey was the skipper for much of the league run, despite knowing he would not be starting the bigger championship games. It was a nod by Gilroy to the veteran Lucan man's loyalty, endurance and influence within the set-up, and was evidence of an evolution in team selection. Gilroy found a way to keep important characters involved on the margins in a manner Caffrey had failed to do. It helped everyone buy in to his message.

'It gave me a new lease of life,' Casey says. 'Ultimately, the big lesson I learned is, a team won't win an All-Ireland, a squad will. Jim Gavin has something similar now and that's what's needed at that level. That's why we didn't have success under previous managers. While we might have had twelve or thirteen good players, ultimately our squad wasn't at that level to compete with the very best.'

Under previous regimes, many of Dublin's players would use their exit from the championship as an opportunity to let loose. The earlier the Dubs went out, the more time they had away from their programmes and the longer it took to get back up to speed for the following season. Defeat was almost a breeding ground for more defeat, a perpetual cycle of just not having enough in the tank to get the job done.

Now, under Gilroy, coming back from a three- or four-month hiatus to begin gym work in December was no longer an option. Strength and conditioning went from a four-month to a twelve-month process. Casey says: 'We'd come back doing gym work in December, then tip over. But lads would have let themselves go quite a bit since September when we weren't training. When you're out of the championship early you have more work to do as a result, to get to the levels required. There's too much to lose if you really let yourself go in that time off. We had more time off, which may have stood against us in that time.'

A surprisingly small crowd, just north of 36,000, turned up to see Dublin lose the league final to Cork by a point, with Mossy Quinn missing two kickable frees late on. Philly McMahon gave no quarter in a tunnel bust-up with Michael Shields, but otherwise Gilroy's men surrendered. An 8-point lead had been swallowed up by the sixty-second minute, before Quinn's late, late horror show. For a side that had been so adept at using the squad, once Bernard Brogan went off injured, joined on the line by Connolly and captain Cullen, they seemed a hollow imitation of themselves. Cork's bench had a greater impact, and they ran out 0-21 to 2-14 winners in a game that bore some painful similarities to the previous season's All-Ireland semi.

Cullen remained as skipper as Dublin clicked into championship gear with a routine 1-16 to 0-11 victory over Laois in the Leinster quarter-final, a game which saw James McCarthy make his championship bow. A 1-12 to 1-11 victory over Kildare set up a Leinster final with Wexford, who had ruthlessly disposed of Carlow in the other semi-final. Just under 44,000 turned up, a consequence of economic devastation and an expectation of a routine win.

Dublin once more found themselves behind with the game in the third quarter. Wexford had done their homework on Cluxton. Wexford boss Jason Ryan felt the keeper was vulnerable to being rounded, and Wexford's forwards were under direct instructions not to shoot if one-on-one, but to try and run around him instead. It worked: with the scores level early in the second half, Redmond Barry danced around Cluxton to score when it might have seemed more straightforward to shoot first time.

'We felt a lot of times, because Cluxton is Cluxton, his reputation gets inside guys' heads,' says Wexford coach John Hegarty. 'So, instead of them focusing on the job in hand, and finishing that, they're sometimes focused on him, and giving him more of an opportunity to stop shots than he should get. I really felt if we got one-on-one and went around him we had a chance.'

Hegarty says they also targeted Cluxton's kick-outs. 'In those days he wasn't lightning fast, but he was very accurate. We'd have spent a portion of training, after we won the semi-final, getting our keepers, showing them in detail where he kicked the ball, and our keepers would be Stephen Cluxton for part of the session.

'Out the field we could arrange where the runners needed to be covered and then we would take ten Dublin kick-outs and look how we were coping with it. Our keepers were good and accurate kickers, so they would put the ball where it needed to be put, to replicate it. So then when it happens in a game people are used to what's coming. We did OK on the day.

'The template that we worked with for Cluxton would have been based on what Mayo were doing. Jason Ryan would have spoken to [Mayo manager] James Horan on it. Mayo were the best and we were trying to replicate what they were doing.'

Gilroy and Cullen went into their opponents' dressing room after the final whistle to commend them on a job well done. Gilroy told them that no team had caused them such problems consistently. He said Dublin were looking at the season starting now, and there was no reason why Wexford couldn't do likewise. Páidí Ó Sé was the only other manager to go into their dressing room after a game, while he was Westmeath boss. He threw them a few unsolicited platitudes, but it was Gilroy's class that left the lasting impression.

Dublin's season was only warming up. On 6 August, they overcame a Tyrone team now in the midst of a steady decline. The 0-22 to 0-15 win saw Diarmuid Connolly come of age as an inter-county star, registering 7 points. Just 52,661 paid in to see it.

The house was almost full three weeks later for the semi-final, one of the most bizarre games ever played in Croke Park and one that left supporters wondering which sport they were watching. It was a battle between two conservative ideologies, the more extreme of which was more unconventional than anything seen before at HQ. Jim McGuinness's Donegal drove down to Dublin and parked a fleet of buses in their own half. They had been starting games slowly to that point in the championship, and they knew what Dublin in full flow were capable of. So they brought down the shutters. From the moment referee Maurice Deegan threw the ball in, yellow shirts began funnelling back towards the Canal end. Colm McFadden and Michael Murphy represented a two-man island off the Donegal mainland, isolated in the Dublin half. Dublin, too, were set up with one eye on containing their opponent first. Half forwards Bryan Cullen and Barry Cahill, both natural defenders, were brought back as always to add cover. The result was isolated attackers, mass defence, messy turnovers, hit-and-hopes, and what RTÉ pundit Colm O'Rourke dubbed the 'game from hell'.

The first point from play arrived in the twenty-fourth minute, when Ryan Bradley put the Ulster champions 0-2 to

0-1 ahead. With roadblocks erected in a congested Donegal half, Dublin's midfield and forwards were starved of space, and decision-making was poor. Diarmuid Connolly, Alan Brogan and Bernard Brogan attempted shots from angles they'd normally only navigate en route to a scoring zone. The Dubs walked into the trap set by their opponents, lumping high balls in to outnumbered forwards who were quickly choked up. In the twenty-eighth minute, Alan Brogan received possession just inside his own half and launched a Hail Mary into land patrolled exclusively by four yellow jerseys. The Dubs failed to score from play in the first half, and went in at the break 0-4 to 0-2 behind.

The small-sided games so central to Mickey Whelan's training were built for days like this. The question was, could Dublin find the key?

Kevin McManamon was the most likely to pick the lock. He was introduced at the break by a manager who knew he had to take the shackles off. But faced with a yellow wall, even he initially struggled to break through. Donegal should have goaled when McFadden was put through just after the restart. He stuck it over. Cluxton put two first-half misses behind him to bring the deficit back to two from a free immediately after, before Donegal went 0-6 to 0-3 in front. Dublin pushed up on their opponents, the defensive cavalry – deemed essential by Gilroy following the Meath shambles in 2010 – clearly not required to cope with Donegal's one-man attack.

Donegal did not score again. 81,436 people had the dubious distinction as being the first to witness a top-level Gaelic football team do nothing more than try to hang on to a three point lead for a half hour. The game plan from the 44th minute onwards seemed about nothing more than ball retention, and by the 50th minute McGuinness's team had amassed an astonishing 200 hand passes and the lion's share of possession – most of it in their own territory. Dublin reduced the deficit to a point courtesy of frees from Bernard Brogan and Cluxton, but on 58 minutes, disaster struck. Connolly won a scoreable free at the Hill 16 end, but instead of taking the chance to equalize, retaliated off the ball and received a harsh red card.

Even with the Dubs down a man, McManamon's direct running started to become a serious problem for Donegal, and on the hour mark he registered the equalizer with Dublin's first point from play. The physical O'Gara came on for James McCarthy as Gilroy sniffed an opportunity. Dublin raised the tempo, and their opponents began to tire.

A man up and with scores level, still Donegal failed to display any attacking urgency or cast off the defensive shackles. Bernard Brogan threaded a sublime ball through the eye of a needle to his captain Cullen on 62 minutes, and Dublin took the lead for the first time. The younger Brogan popped over another free six minutes later to effectively seal it. He failed to score from play, but from limited possession turned provider in a display that marked a new kind of game intelligence.

Gilroy's men saw out a game they struggled for so long in easily, and were back in a final for the first time in 16 years. Their first-half showing, when they played the game on their opponent's terms, was poor, but they did not panic, and their tactics and decision-making improved after the break. It was a dirty game that Dublin sides of the preceding decade and a half would have found a way to lose. When it mattered the most, in the cauldron of championship football, Dublin displayed a new resilience in the face of adversity. Their supreme fitness levels, physical and mental, helped grind out a most unusual victory. It was ugly, but it infused the players with the sort of belief that a routine win never could.

The result left Dublin in unfamiliar territory. The third Sunday in September was rapidly approaching, and they were still in the championship, Kerry the only team left standing in Gilroy's way.

Dublin supporters knew how to fill Croke Park. But the Leinster championship, even an All-Ireland-semi, is one thing; accessing tickets for a final is a different beast entirely. The Dubs, whose minors were also in action that day against Tipperary, were allocated 18,000 tickets for the final, Kerry 11,000. Supporters who in the past had no problems snapping up tickets on general sale suddenly found themselves in the scrap of their lives. Bereft fans vented against the unfairness of it, railing against the bandwagoners and corporate elite. Touts were flogging tickets for up to a grand on eBay. Well-known members of the Hill 16 army, including eighty-year-old Tony Broughan, spent the week before the game begging anyone and everyone for goodwill. Tony, who decks himself out as Molly Malone and had been going to Dublin matches for seventy years, issued a plea through the papers. Bertie Ahern was inundated with requests, but wasn't impressed with their pedigree. He said: 'Eighty per cent of those who come after you, looking for tickets for the All-Ireland, if you directed them to Parnell Park they'd probably go to the Parnell monument!'

It was the final the neutrals wanted to see, and it was hard to escape the intense build-up. 1970s hero Keaveney was on his annual pilgrimage to the Listowel races days before the big game, where even his iconic status couldn't save him from the taunts of anyone who recognized him. In Skerries Harps

GAA club, home of Dubs skipper Cullen, chairman Niall Murphy from Tralee found himself torn between county allegiances and his own club's date with destiny. Former Dr Crokes keeper Peter O'Brien, the man who christened Colm Cooper 'the Gooch', chose the week of the game to reveal that the nickname referred to a red-haired doll he'd seen for sale in a Killarney market, which gave the Hill something to work with on match day. 'Sam is Coming Home' got a 2011 revamp, too. Eoghan O'Gara, who became a dad for the first time in the week before the final, had been removed from the song's lyrics earlier in the summer after picking up an injury. It didn't sit too well with the Templeogue wrecking ball, and when he bumped into the composer afterwards he told him as much. 'He was only half joking,' says Liam.

But not everyone got into the swing of the final. When Labour TD Aodhán Ó Ríordáin drove into the grounds of Leinster House with Dublin flags flying from his car, he was ordered to take them down: there was a flag ban. The Scoil Uí Chonaill clubman moaned: 'I could come into the Dail chamber in full Dublin kit and nobody would do anything as there's no dress code, but they made me take my flags down. I put them back as soon as I got out of the car park, obviously.'

When Gooch lashed over two in a row to put Kerry 1-10 to 0-9 ahead on sixty-three minutes, it felt as though a familiar script was playing itself out again.

A minute later, Alan Brogan fed Kevin McManamon, and a cult hero was born when the super-sub rounded a Kerry defender and blasted the ball into the net. In the blink of a disbelieving eye, wing back Kevin Nolan swung over his first-ever championship point from thirty-five metres, and Dublin were level. And then Bernard Brogan, working like for most of his career he didn't know he could, nailed a huge point on sixty-nine minutes to put Dublin in front.

MacAuley put one wide, before Kieran Donaghy down the Canal End put a monster kick into the sky. By the time it eventually fell, it was over Stephen Cluxton's crossbar and the Kingdom were level. Ger Brennan won a free for Dublin, and then lost it again by sticking his palm in Donaghy's face. The hop fell kindly to Dublin, and the ball found its way into the hands of McManamon, who was bundled over. Free in. Bernard Brogan beckoned Stephen Cluxton towards the kick that would define his career and perhaps the rest of his life. It was located almost forty-five yards out, to the right-hand side of the posts, facing into Hill 16.

Cluxton, a man with 15 career points to his name at that point, had taken this kick thousands of times before. He'd done it in his head, he'd done it on the training pitch, he'd even done it here in Croker. He stepped up. Time stood still, just for a moment, and hazy snapshots of the past came into sharp focus. Sixteen years of hurt, ready to be expunged with one kick. In their mind's eye supporters could see an older Croke Park, a decaying Hogan Stand which was then a reflection of their team's decline. Shane Ryan, Ciaran Whelan, Collie Moran, Paddy Christie, Ray Cosgrove – warriors all – had never experienced a moment like this.

Cluxton didn't miss, and seconds later, as the final whistle blew, Croke Park heard noise that until then had existed only in dreams.

Supporters wept behind the Hill 16 Perspex as the players struggled to grasp the scale of their achievement. Dublin hadn't beaten Kerry when it mattered since 1977, and yet here they were, like master pickpockets, having stolen victory from the unlikeliest victim.

Pillar Caffrey, on duty in full Garda uniform, embraced the players he'd brought so close. Casey was in tears, as much for his own achievement and for that of his teammates as for the players who had gone before. The All-Ireland victory belonged to everyone, and he was happy to share it.

Gilroy hugged his children as skipper Bryan Cullen took Sam in his hands and pointed him towards the sky. He told the world that they had been to 'hell and back' in their odyssey to the top of those steps, before declaring: 'See you all in Coppers!' And once the party in the hotel was wrapped up, see them in Coppers the players did, joined by more than one stalwart of the past. The squad's best singers, including Kev Mac, found a kindred spirit in balladeer Damien Dempsey as they partied into the early morning. At the Boar's Head pub the following morning, the players were joined by Senator David Norris, not particularly renowned for his own singing exploits. The Sunnybank wasn't forgotten either. John McCarthy took Rory O'Carroll to his old watering hole for a late-night celebratory scoop, decades after it all began for him there.

For the retired players who missed out, there was joy as well. It was, naturally enough, tinged with regret, the feeling of what might have been. In the glow of victory, the All-Ireland winners felt for their former colleagues too. Casey felt it when he met Collie Moran.

'When you're involved with those fellas and you know those fellas, you were involved in dressing rooms and know the commitment that was given . . . Sometimes I look back at the Pillar era and you nearly think the squad became that much closer because we weren't having that All-Ireland success. Unfortunately we fell short, but that bond you'll never lose and I'll never fail to acknowledge that with old teammates as well.' In the aftermath, MacAuley was just one player who offered a grateful nod to the veterans who had rolled with the punches for years before making their breakthrough. 'I'm happier more for them than myself,' he said.

In Ahern's eyeline when Cullen raised Sam aloft was Enda Kenny, and the Dub felt a small pang of regret. 'I would have loved to be Taoiseach, to bring them in with the cup, but you know I was there for eleven years and they didn't win it. Winning was the most important thing.' Bertie had been given a standing ovation in Parnell Park the Sunday after he quit as Taoiseach in 2008. But on the evening of 18 September, in the hours after watching his beloved Dubs win their first title in sixteen years, he was derided by some supporters in his local, Fagan's. The post-crash pain being felt by ordinary people was particularly acute around that time, and Ahern bore the brunt of that. Time would heal some of those wounds, but it wasn't the perfect ending he had envisaged.

'My relationship with Dubs fans now is great,' he says. 'You get a few lads who wouldn't know anything about Dublin, the kind of guys who joined in when Shamrock Rovers were doing well thirty years ago, but most supporters were very good to me. I remember the ovation [in 2008]. I really appreciated it. They're great supporters. The bandwagoners can be a problem but by and large the fans are great.'

Those who knew Cluxton insist the script was written for the enigmatic goalie. Anyone outside his circle who hoped to get to know the Parnells man would be disappointed: he didn't want them to get to know him. Sometimes cranky, sometimes full of craic, the secondary school teacher was resolute in his determination to stay who he was. His contrariness and occasional meltdowns weren't confined to the GAA pitch: just a few months earlier he had been sent off for swiping at former Irish soccer international Jason McAteer in a charity match. The bizarre incident piqued the interest of the media, but while his colleagues including Bernard Brogan, Barry Cahill and Paul Flynn all had their say, Cluxton kept quiet.

He did an interview once, for Dave Berry's documentary of the Dubs' 2005 season. He talked about how celebrations weren't for him, so he left the team to mark their Leinster title victory over Laois and cup presentation to go sit in the dressing room. 'I'm out there to play football and that's really all it is. It's nothing else,' he said. Six years and a few crucial months later, after the final whistle had blown on the final, Cluxton was back in the dressing room getting his boots off while the team saluted their fans. No fuss. At that moment he might have been preparing mentally for work in St Vincent's in Glasnevin the following morning, had his principal not forced him to take the day off. It wasn't often Stephen Cluxton did anything against his will, but in the end it was just as well he did. After a night without sleep he was with his Dublin colleagues, kicking off a tradition that would see them start the day after All-Ireland final day drinking pints – or in his case, blue WKD – in the Boar's Head.

'If they asked you after he got the winning point in an All-Ireland final how he's going to react, you'd say Stephen is going to be Stephen,' smiles Casey. 'He can be cranky, Stephen, when he wants to be, he can be Stephen full of craic. That's just who he is. And in fairness, he'll never change. While it may have changed other people if they were in that situation, he will never change. He doesn't let it go to his head, he'll just go out the next day and work hard again.

'He ultimately typifies this current Dublin team and he keeps a lot of fellas' feet on the ground. It's not stuff he does, it's how he acts and how he goes about his business. He doesn't have to say too much, but when he does talk people listen.'

Dublin didn't quite know what to do with Sam Maguire. The old boy didn't have a diary, and nor did his secret body-double. It took a while for him to get into a routine, but before long he was hopping around from club to club, re-tracing the steps of yore with handlers for a new generation. In the weeks after the September success, many of the players took a trip to the United States, where they played second fiddle to their famous new companion. The Friends of Dublin GAA in Boston – those friends were everywhere by now – arranged to bring Gilroy over with players including the Brogans, MacAuley, Fitzsimons, O'Carroll and Casey.

Also in town was Moran, that soldier of so many campaigns, perhaps robbed of his big shot by injury two years earlier. Speaking to his old pal David Henry at the bar, he pointed in Gilroy's direction and said: 'He did well, didn't he?' Henry responded: 'That fella could run the country.'

'I thought it was a good line,' says Moran. 'The IMF were in town back home and the country was going through a lot of stuff. But the more I thought about it, Pat had proven himself to be a very pragmatic and successful businessman. Then he came in as Dublin senior football manager when the county was probably on a bit of a low – and with basically no prior managerial experience. Yet here he was with Sam Maguire in Boston. He was a man who got things done.'

It took a while, and there were many more characters in addition to Pat Gilroy who sweated blood and tears over sixteen years to get them there. The vast majority of them were no longer involved. But whether they were there in body or only in spirit, every last one of them got there in the end.

14. The Fans

Few forget their first day on Hill 16. The concrete mass at the Railway end was colonized by Dublin supporters in the 1970s and, despite efforts at infiltration over the years by outside forces, it has remained largely blue ever since. It has been at times violent, and filthy. Rivers of urine once flowed down the steps with more force than the waters of the nearby Tolka. It's been unwelcoming, it's been brutal. It's been loud, and it's been quiet. It's a breeding ground for comedians. There is nothing else quite like it in GAA. There's no great science to Hill 16, but a few rules usually apply.

1. Young lads going for the first time with their dads take their place to the top left third looking down on the pitch, adjacent to the Cusack Stand. Taller people will always stand in their way. In days of pre-development yore, the smallest children would arrive four hours before throw-in and take their spot behind the old exit walls, guaranteeing themselves an unobstructed view of the pitch. That is, unless some bigger boys came along and encouraged them to move. Older men and women also congregate here. It's the Hill, only with a bit of comfort, like having pre-boarding on a Ryanair flight to Magaluf.

2. As the youngfellas grow a few inches and become less reliant on Dad, they'll skip the middle third

entirely and head for the area directly behind the goal. This is now effectively the first third, although it used to be the middle before the changes. (There may be numbers and letters on the steps these days, but we don't talk in technical terms. Try to keep up.) These lads will normally have a few cans of cider stuffed down their pants, even in these times of heightened security. A few will have flags. There used to be more, but Croke Park don't want flags on Hill 16. Health and safety. They get the chants going, their voices lubricated by the Bulmers.

3. The middle third is where the greying, balding and sagging cohort go. These people can be of a certain vintage, or merely have been around too long to stand behind the goal. They like a song too, but are a bit more reserved. If they don't catch on to the 'Come . . . on . . . ' emanating from the youths, there's a chance the crew of Dad and children over on the top left, effectively deafened to the chant by wind direction, will start their own separate song and leave the confused middle crew with a choice to make.

4. Thankfully, the song is always 'Come . . . on . . . you . . . boys in blue', so it's only a matter of fusing the outer thirds and bringing the chorus in sync. Occasionally, a few lads try 'Molly Malone', but that always gets a mixed response at best. The guy who sang 'Who's your father, who's your father, who's your father referee, you haven't got one, you never had one, you're a bastard referee' got a few laughs, but no backing choir.

5. Nobody ever wants to stand on the Nally terrace. That's the bit to the far side, touching the Hogan Stand and sloping in under that weird box that hangs there. It's boring, and most real fans who end up with Nally tickets will either scale the fence into the Hill or else chance their arm getting in through the Hill turnstile. Both have worked. The Nally terrace used to be the Nally Stand, a charming little place reserved for pensioners. That tells you all you need to know about that place.

6. Experienced Hill-goers know exactly what the stewards are doing when they say there's plenty of room to get in through Gate A. Gate A means you're being pigeonholed into the area for kids and oldies, touching the Cusack. That is precisely why there is always plenty of room. Dubs fans in Caffrey's time especially developed a reputation for having that last pint and forcing the delay of throw-in. The accepted wisdom is that Croke Park's cunning Gate A plan was a way of eliminating the late arrivals. It has largely worked.

7. If you want to sell a few bodhrans, there's a small but significant market on Hill 16.

8. At the end of every game, fans emerging from each of the exits into the bowels of the stadium will launch into a rendition of 'We're going to win the Sam', rarely if ever with even a hint of sarcasm.

9. Supporters from other counties occasionally made their way on to the Hill in the 1990s and 2000s. They were always rounded upon and ridiculed, but

the abuse was always 'good-natured' – even if it cut the recipients to the very core of their being. 'Get off the Hill' was the message.

10. The Perspex at the front of the terrace, we presume, is to keep us penned in like animals because that is, we presume, how we are seen.

Hill 16 is no picnic, but for tens of thousands of the Dublin contingent, there is nowhere else they would rather be. Kevin Heffernan's revolution brought the colour to the terraces, and the supporters have jealously guarded their right to stand there ever since. Rival supporters who tried to stand with them were rebuffed, as were efforts by the authorities to put seats down.

It's a much safer place now than it was in the days when idiots would rain glass bottles down on to their own fellow-supporters, or pull knives. That sort of crap was rare, because most fans wouldn't tolerate it. The Hill was about standing your ground, summoning all your reserves of strength just to keep your feet planted on the ground as the heave from behind threatened to suck you into the air.

It was also about looking out for the guy beside you. Strangers are friends, unless the stranger is the gobshite who spends seventy minutes abusing his own players. That guy is always there, dotted around the terrace like a plague of tiny cold sores. He's one type, but there are others.

1. The Know It All. The guy who knew a player was coming through before his own manager did. The guy who could tell you how well Thomas Davis were going in the league, or how St Brigid's were having a shocker this year. He's not a man who likes

to keep his thoughts to himself, no matter how hard his neighbours will it on him. 'I've been watchin' [insert name here] since he was seven and I'm tellin' ya he has a chance.'

2. The Drunken Bozo. He won't know who we're playing or even where he is, necessarily, and will challenge the people around him to 'fuckin' sing you dopes.' 'Come . . . on . . . zzzzzz.'

3. The Gossip. He's the fella who tells everyone that the centre half forward's wife is having a fling with a lad from Ballinteer St John's. 'He wasn't at training on Thursday night, they're at marriage counselling. My cousin is the counsellor.'

4. The True Blue. He will remind you, just in case you're in any doubt, that he was in Tralee for the league game, and was up in Drogheda for the O'Byrne Cup opener. 'See that wide there? He did the exact same thing in Clones in the league.'

5. The Wise Old Sage. He might not be too old, but by God is he wise. He won't say much, but when he says it, people listen. He's normally stuck beside the True Blue or the Drunken Bozo, but he always keeps his dignity. His deliveries are always sharp and to the point. When he does open his mouth, it tends to mean something. 'Beware the Ides of March,' he'll say, just before Dublin are turned over in injury time.

Hill 16 isn't just the terrace, it's also the collective. Hill 16 is in Parnell Park, Páirc Uí Rinn, Breffni Park, Castlebar and

Páirc Tailteann. It's wherever the Dubs are. If Dublin's footballers are the heart and soul of that togetherness, Hill 16 in full voice is the lung.

Disappointment has at times bred a strange contentment, the knowledge that we are in this together, no matter what's thrown at us. Winning doesn't always sit well. The detractors talk about cocky Dubs, but that arrogance is a mask. It's in defeat where the wit is sharpest, the band of brothers and sisters standing firm against a biting wind.

Epilogue: Finishing Up

Inter-county players are amateurs, but we treat them like professionals. The sacrifices they make are often overlooked. The guy who gets ridiculed for missing that late chance to win a game may have forfeited a professional career, and neglected family and relationships, in order to pursue a sporting dream. When the end comes – and the end always comes – some players realize they have given up their youth for a fishbowl pursuit that doesn't always bear fruit.

For some, the end comes easily enough. Others never even see it coming.

'I came on against Tyrone in the drawn game in 2005 and done particularly well,' says Darren Homan. 'I was just starting to work in the Fire Brigade at the time, and Dessie said to me, "I've been talking to Pillar, he says you're starting next week." I told him, "I'm in work Saturday, I won't get across." He said, "Do your best." So I got time off and went across to training that day, and that's when I picked up the injury.'

Homan had an accidental training-ground clash with Ciaran Whelan and injured his back. He had been doing what he loved. And then, a few days before one of the biggest games of his life, he was finished.

'I suppose I was lucky at the time – I wasn't too long in the Fire Brigade. With them you're rostered days and you're rostered nights. I would have been training every night with the lads, and then you're going in to work with the same seventeen or eighteen fellas, so there was that same kind of camaraderie. The Fire Brigade gave me a different impetus.

'And then, a year or two later, my son Sean was born and that kind of kept me busy from then on. But it's a huge culture shock.'

Pillar threw him a party, and Homan was delighted to see the younger players he liked to look out for turn up to give him a send-off. It helped ease the pain a little. From then on he'd be watching those players from afar, a keen observer, interested to see if they'd go as far as he thought they would.

Homan, like most players, built up close bonds with teammates over the years. For the most part, however, when it's over, it's over. People fall out of touch, the phone stops ringing, and you're on your own. Homan struggles to identify *his* team now. He didn't win an All-Ireland. When a team wins nothing, where are the bonds that can tie them together?

'I was very pally with the likes of Ciaran Whelan and Collie Moran, when we were training. Collie I'm still in touch with, but I don't really hear from the other lads any more, you know? I'd get the odd text.

'While you're training hard, you're having great craic. Your teammates were your best friends because you didn't really go to clubs, you didn't socialize, you didn't do this or that, because you were dedicated. You were training, not drinking. Saturday mornings, Sunday mornings, whatever it was, so you see more of each other than your family.'

When it's over, the player has to spend some time trying to find his place in the old order. To see if he belongs anywhere.

It would have been easier, Homan thinks, for guys who had been on the 1995 team. 'They'll always be brought back to do fan events or whatever because they won the All-Ireland. One of the biggest regrets, after working and training so hard with the lads, the blood sweat and tears that you shed together, is that we can't come together to look at each other on a night out years later, to know that you have that medal in your back pocket. That would have made it all worth it, I suppose.'

After a long time on the sidelines, and an operation on his back, Homan wanted to get back on the pitch. 'You say in the back of your mind you want to play football again. Because I hadn't played the year before, I was entitled to play junior.' The Dublin junior panel that won the All-Ireland title in 2008, under Mick Deegan, included Michael Fitzsimons, Eoghan O'Gara, Denis Bastick, Darren Daly and Jonny Cooper. Against Roscommon in the final, Homan was sprung from the bench and made the impact that was expected of him: he ruffled a few feathers and scored a point.

He felt, though, that he was a marked man. 'I used to be a hard, dirty player. Because I was an ex-Dublin [senior] player, I'd go out to play a match, and people would be looking to have a crack off you because of who you played for. By 2008 I wasn't the Darren Homan of a couple of years ago, where I loved to fight or bash them off the ball or whatever. I was only going out for a game of football and I didn't want to get myself hurt – it wasn't worth it any more. I called it a day a month after the junior final.'

Paddy Christie went with even less fuss. The Hill 16 darling shuffled off at the end of the 2006 season, in which he hadn't played much. He had his teaching, and his coaching. For a man who shunned the glitzy side of being an inter-county star anyway, it was an easy enough call when his body stopped obeying orders. He was one of the lucky ones.

'It took me a long time to get back to where I wanted to

get to, following a Gilmore's groin op in January. So automatically my thoughts were to move on. I thought that was enough for me, I was pretty ruthless and selfish, I wasn't doing it for the good of Dublin football.

'I'd come from nowhere. Nobody knew anything about me. I was playing, and then in the evenings or the summer I worked in Superquinn in Finglas. Nobody knew who I was; a few knew I played for Kickhams minors, that's about it. I went around the shop and the area, my parents kept to themselves, we weren't going around with a famous family heritage. Then I was suddenly on the team doing well for myself.

'So I never had that pressure of being touted for years. Then when it was over, I sort of disappeared out of existence again. I came out of nowhere and went straight back. Life just went on. I'd love to be back at nineteen again and would do a few things differently, but would do most of it the same. I enjoyed playing, the big days were fantastic, but life has to move on. I remember walking out of Croke Park in 2006, we'd been beaten by Mayo, and I said, "I think that's it for me now. I can take or leave this, I've had enough."

'Someone asked me months later was I retired, and I just said, "I'm not available at the moment." Pillar rang me, said, "We're gonna be bringing in new fellas, what's your thoughts?" I said, "I'm happy enough at the club, obviously if I come back and play unbelievable football and miss it so much I'll ring you back." But I never did. Most of the things I did over the years I got right. When leaving Croke Park that day, we'd been beaten and it was a sickener; even though I didn't play I felt bad for the rest of the lads, I knew how they felt because I'd had those defeats.

'I think it's horrible when I see people going around, longing to be back, because you're never going to be back there, you know? It's never going to happen, those days are gone. If I was to think about it too much, it would put me into a depression. It's a different phase of your life. I have two young kids now, I have to look after them. I'm vice-principal [at Our Lady of Victories national school in Ballymun], training Ballymun seniors, U-21 manager and I train the Trinity Sigerson Cup team. I managed Dublin minors for a few years.

'Coming from nowhere made it easier to go back to nothing. I was never made a big deal of. When I was finished I went back to being an ordinary Joe Soap and life goes on. My mother's family are from Lorrha in Tipperary, a very rural area near Portumna. Mad hurling fanatics. My cousin was on the Tipp minor footballers on the same year I didn't make Dublin. Nobody even mentioned me.'

Eamon Heery's career as a Dublin senior footballer lasted almost a decade, with 1995 falling in the middle of it – and yet he departed without the Celtic cross in his pocket. His playing days finished in the late 1990s, a time when the preparation that goes into the game was a world away from what it is today. He wouldn't swap it.

'The likes of Mick Kennedy never got his due reward either. As I say to my young fella, we competed with the best, that's all you can say. They were the best. Marking Colm O'Rourke and Bernard Flynn. David Beggy, fuck me. Dave Barry from Cork, and Dinny Allen. You pitted yourself against the best, that's all you can do. It's up to other people to decide whether you did well or not.

'You go down the country, you see guys you played against years ago and you have a few pints. That's not bad, is it? I don't see Barrsy for six or eight months then you go for a few pints, you don't want to be in each other's ear either! We meet up for a few after a match, just like we went for a few pints after training on a Thursday. You don't have that now, of course. I wouldn't like to be a player now, I don't know how they live their lives. They're a different breed.

'Barrsy always said to me, "Heery, we won fuck-all, but we had great craic."'

He could have been speaking for most of them.

Acknowledgements

All I knew when I began working on this book is that I wanted to write about a period of time that was immensely frustrating as a supporter, and yet oddly rewarding. The gallows humour that sustained us through the bad times has disappeared in this time of plenty, and in a weird way I miss it.

I want to thank Keith Barr, Eamon Heery, Paul Clarke, Paddy Christie, Johnny Magee, Ray Cosgrove, Mick O'Keeffe, John O'Leary, Tom Carr, Tommy Lyons, Mark Vaughan, Paul Casey, Darren Homan, Shane Ryan and Collie Moran for sharing their often painful memories and for being so generous with their time. Thanks too to Graham Geraghty, Justin McNulty, Fergal Byron and John Hegarty, who contributed fantastic insight on what it was like to play against Dublin. Many thanks also to John Bailey and Bertie Ahern for sharing their thoughts on the major events of that time. Thank you to Mick Garvey and Sean Garvey for their memories of the Sunnybank Hotel, and to Liam and Eoghan Heneghan of The Merry Ploughboy. A number of people spoke to me off the record and gave me helpful steers, and I would like to thank them too.

Thanks to Cathal Dervan for putting me in touch with Penguin, and to Michael McLoughlin for taking a chance on the project. Also to my editor Brendan Barrington, who managed to prevent me repeating myself over and over again and who endured several emails a day. Many people proved invaluable with numbers and contacts, including Gordon Manning, Jason Byrne, Ken Bogle, Barry Moran, Ruairi Cotter, David

McManus and Alan Hartnett, while Bryan O'Higgins, John Kelly, Paul Stafford and Jude Bredin were always full of encouragement (!). Thanks to Chris Doyle, who sorted out the photographs for me. My editor in the *Irish Sun*, Donegal man Kieran McDaid, was very understanding when I needed to duck out for something Dubs-related, and colleague Mark May was great at picking up the slack when my mind was elsewhere. Also a nod to Karl Deeter, Stephen Breen and Owen Conlon for their advice on what's involved in writing and publishing a book.

My late dad Liam is the reason I started following Dublin in the first place. His enthusiasm was infectious and his ability to land an All-Ireland final ticket from nowhere the reason we rarely missed a game. He passed away in 1998, during one of those frustrating summers. That year he had gone to herbalist – and scourge of Dublin – Sean Boylan for alternative remedies. The Meath GAA legend did some great work for him, and when my dad asked how much he owed him, Sean insisted that if he switched allegiances to the Royals it was on the house. 'Not a hope!' was the response. Boylan laughed and refused to charge him.

Thanks to Ciaran, Maebh, and my mam Yvonne: I know this probably isn't the book she originally had in mind, but she's always been a great encouragement. My uncle Gerry's treasure trove of match-day programmes got the ball rolling for me, while his wife Ann and son Paul were always full of helpful suggestions. Clare and Joe endured much of the miserable times on Hill 16 with us, and their pre-match fry-ups continue to sustain us.

Hopefully the good times won't stop rolling for a while. But when they do, we'll be ready for it.

Select Bibliography

Match-day programmes collected between 1992 and 2005 were a great source of information, helping with team selections (they were printed accurately on the match-day programme in those days), results, match reports and league tables. And the following articles and books were very helpful.

Books

Breheny, Martin & John O'Leary, *Back to the Hill: The Official Biography*, Blackwater Press, 1997

Corry, Eoghan, *Deadlock: Dublin vs Meath 1991*, Gill & Macmillan, 2011

Farrell, Dessie & Sean Potts, *Tangled Up in Blue*, Town House, 2005

Hayes, Liam, *Heffo: A Brilliant Mind*, Transworld Ireland, 2013

Leonard, John, *Dub Sub Confidential*, Penguin, 2015

Sherlock, Jason, Jayo: *The Jason Sherlock Story*, Simon & Schuster, 2017

Reports

Anon., 'Annual Report for the Irish Sports Council 2014', GAA Games Development, 2014

Anon., 'Irish Sports Monitor 2015 Annual Report', Spórt Éireann, 2015

Newspapers

Anon., 'Tense time for Dublin's prince and their prince in waiting', *The Irish Times*, 14 June 1997

Anon., 'A blue day as Dubs roll into town', *Longford Leader*, 3 June 2016

Breheny, Martin, 'Dublin's Blue Book quote fits for Mayo's long wait', *Irish Independent*, 15 September 2017

Brogan, Alan, 'Meath humiliation in 2010 was turning point for Dublin', *Evening Herald*, 23 June 2016

Cunningham, Kieran, 'How Dublin breed footballers', *Buzz.ie*, 6 September 2016

——, 'Vinnie, vidi, vici – the life and times of King of the Hill', *Buzz.ie*, 9 April 2017

Hancock, Ciaran, 'Dublin GAA scores with €6million Vodafone deal', *Irish Times*, 11 December 2009

Kelly, Niall, 'Gilroy pulling the strings on Brogan's star turn', *the42.ie*, 7 June 2012

Keys, Colm, 'Pillars of consistency', *Irish Independent*, 22 August 2007

——, 'Dublin's biggest gamble', *Irish Independent*, 10 October 2008

Lawlor, Damian, 'Pillar's pyramid of coaches', *Irish Independent*, 15 July 2007

Manning, Gordon, 'Serious operator', *Irish Sun*, 29 September 2017

Moran, Sean, 'Carr gets green light as Dublin manager', *Irish Times*, 9 December 1997

——, 'Big bang of 2009 created Dublin's new football universe', *Irish Times*, 13 September 2017

O'Connor, Christy, 'Stephen Cluxton, the man behind the icy image', *Irish Independent*, 24 September 2011

Rowe, Simon, 'From sporting glory to boardroom success', *Irish Independent*, 24 September 2016

Shannon, Kieran, 'Coaches find their time and place at last', *Irish Examiner*, 13 September 2011

——, 'Mickey Whelan has had a huge impact on GAA', *Irish Examiner*, 27 March 2017

Slattery, Will, 'Caffrey is content to be a face in the crowd', *Irish Independent*, 15 September 2017

Index